Lessons for the Stage

The Little Foxes by Lillian Hellman

Lessons for the Stage

An Approach to Acting

by Julian S. Schlusberg

With an Afterword by Howard Stein

Archon Books Hamden, Connecticut 1994

This Book Donated By:
Sheila Kennedy

First published 1994 by Archon Books,

an imprint of The Shoe String Press, Inc.,

Hamden, Connecticut 06514.

Library of Congress Cataloging-in-Publication Data

Schlusberg, Julian S., 1947–

Lessons for the stage: an approach to acting /

by Julian Schlusberg.

p.   cm.

Includes bibliographical references.

ISBN 0-208-02373-9 (alk. paper)

1. Acting—Study and teaching.   2. College and

school drama, American.   3. Youth as actors.

I. Title

PN2075.S345   1994

792'.028'07—dc 20   93-37695

                                  CIP

The photographs here are of the author's
play productions at Hamden High School,
Hamden, Connecticut.

The paper in this publication meets the minimum
requirements of American National Standard for
Information Science—Permanence of Paper for Printed
Library Materials, ANSI Z39.48–1984. ⊗

Printed in the United States of America

For my mother and father

"We all know that something is eternal, and it ain't names and it ain't houses and it ain't earth and it ain't even the stars. There's something eternal about every human being."—Thornton Wilder

Contents

*A lesson designated by an asterisk may be used
 independently of lesson groups.

Acknowledgments

I am forever indebted to the late Constance Welch, a brilliant teacher who, under George Pierce Baker, was instrumental in founding the Yale School of Drama. Although this celebrated teacher, coach, and director produced students who became, over the course of some fifty years, leaders of the American Theater, one would hardly know it when looking at this unassuming, modest, gentle woman. Roderick Bladel, who dedicated his book, *Walter Kerr's Analysis and Criticism,* to Miss Welch, said ". . . she made acting *feel* so good. The best I've ever felt, the most fulfilled, was when I was acting under her guidance." This sentiment is shared by many, as is the feeling that we were somehow blessed to be taught by her.

For some reason quite unknown to me, my path has rather miraculously crossed those of other people who, through their wisdom and the humility integral to that wisdom, have affected me greatly. Among those are Howard Stein, a man who knows more about theater than anyone I know and who imparts that knowledge with inspiration and love; the late Shakespearean scholar Leslie Hotson and his wife, Mary; Dr. Robert E. Kendall and A. Richard Coakley of Southern Connecticut State University, both of whom are with me spiritually if not in person any more; and Anthony Mark Watts, an acting teacher, director, mentor, and friend. I thank these, my teachers, and hope I have been worthy of the gifts they have bestowed upon me.

I am especially grateful to my students through the years, a truly exceptional "family" of human beings. Many have gone on to professional theater, many have become teachers of theater, and many have used theater skills in their varied occupations. All of them, however, are bonded in their love for our art and their admiration and respect for each other. To have worked, learned, and shared with them has been so rewarding! How wealthy I am to have taught these wonderful people who are "touching" the world in a special way.

I would also like to thank the Hamden (Connecticut) Public School System for its commitment to educational theater. In times when investment in the arts is being minimized and in some cases erased completely, Hamden continues to demonstrate its faith in the importance of the arts in education. I am proud to work in a town with such vision.

I am thankful to Jim and Diantha Thorpe and their staff at The Shoe

String Press for believing in this project. Their understanding, patience, warmth, and enthusiasm are greatly appreciated. And I thank Karen Burgess, a longtime friend, who so beautifully illustrated the charts in this book.

And finally, I thank those who have been so important in my personal life—my family and friends who are treasured beyond words. The "secret of life" is loving them.

J.S.

A Note to the Teacher

Teaching acting is one of the greatest joys in the world! I'm sure most drama teachers share that sentiment, although, if asked to explain why, we might be at a loss for words. Hopefully, we have all experienced that thrill of watching our students perform masterfully in major productions, when the nuances of gesture and voice worked together to create some truly fine acting. Hopefully, we have also witnessed that secretly longed-for rehearsal moment when an actor suddenly and magically "understands"—like Helen in *The Miracle Worker*—and is transformed before our eyes into Regina in Lillian Hellman's *The Little Foxes*, or Iago in Shakespeare's *Othello*, or Eliza in Barrie's *The Admirable Crichton*. These moments are indescribable—uplifting and poignant. They seem to, in an instant, outweigh the tremendous amounts of time and energy we must find to mount a production. When our colleagues ask us how we can possibly devote that much time, how do we find the words to describe the exhilaration of such moments? How do we convince them that "time" is insignificant compared to what we receive in return?

But we must never neglect the *process* as we pursue the *product*, for the process is a special time indeed: a time of growth and self-awareness, a time of decision-making and the discovery of options, a time of fun and camaraderie and sharing and trusting and learning responsibility, yet also a time of discipline and obeying the rules.

I firmly believe that theater education should occupy an important place in the contemporary curriculum, and enlightened individuals—superintendents, principals, teachers, and students—have gone to great lengths and taken great risks to convince the educational community, as well as the community at large, of this.

We acting teachers are different from our more competition-minded colleagues in that our training is not forced to the test on the football field, in the hockey rink, or on the SATs. Our students do not have to perform in major productions to take advantage of the wealth of knowledge offered in our acting classes. Critical thinking skills, conceptualization, and application of theory, as well as poise, self-confidence, self-discovery, and self-esteem, are just as integral to the development of our students in class as they are to those who perform in polished, costumed productions. And while we should, needless to say, continue to strive for top-notch, high-quality productions, our value to the educational system should not be based solely on this aspect of our work. Our job must be recognized for its impact on *all* students in our programs, and not only on those who participate in after-school drama activities.

The acting class is many things to many students. Some use it as a step in professional training; many want to learn about the art form itself; some use it as a method of securing a good role in an upcoming production; some want to improve communication skills needed for other professions; and still others want to "test the waters," so to speak—to see what this "acting thing" is all about. What all want in common, however, is simply an enjoyable learning experience. It is my hope that this book will help to provide that.

Lessons for the Stage is meant to be a very practical guide to meet the needs of all kinds of students. Acting classes, in my experience, are often composed of mixed grade levels and of high and low academic achievers, of different types of learners with varying degrees of outward enthusiasm. Theater students and aspiring actors are inherently a diverse group. I have used the same lessons successfully with adult night classes that I have used with a special education class made up of behaviorally and emotionally disturbed high school students. This heterogeneity is wonderful. The commonality is provided by subject matter; the richness is provided by the diverse backgrounds of the participants.

I feel that the two levels of acting treated here should be taught in a somewhat less formal manner than most academic subjects, yet both should be highly disciplined courses. Participants should have the utmost respect for each other and their differences. The "right-wrong" approach is suitable only for objective aspects of training: stage left is *not* stage right. Otherwise it should be replaced by freedom of interpretation and the sharing of choices. Classes should be marked by activity and stimulating discussion, and the students should feel comfortable asking questions and expressing their opinions openly. If active involvement is *encouraged*, everyone is likely to benefit from the resulting diversity, which will certainly include many forms of ignorance and nonsense—including those of the teacher—because we are dealing with a structured process which encourages choices, sharing, cooperation, responsibility, and the "right" to be "wrong."

Our job carries enormous responsibility. If I were to summarize the requirements of an acting teacher I would say *expertise*, *tact*, and *sensitivity*. Students really need to trust an acting teacher, to rely on that teacher's knowledge and good judgment, sense of fairness, and dignity. To make oneself vulnerable before a class/audience, as we do in the performance fields, is difficult enough, but to be embarrassed through the teacher's mishandling of an assignment or critique can cause irreparable harm to a student's personal growth.

I hope you will find *Lessons for the Stage* a valuable book. I have had the privilege of witnessing some pretty remarkable work based on these lessons. I've also had the privilege of witnessing the maturation of many wonderful students who have, over both courses, developed their creativity, sense of self, and sensitivity to others and to their environment.

Author's note: I wish our language had one all-encompassing pronoun with which to refer to all of the readers of this book. As it does not, the use of the masculine pronoun is meant to include everyone. I sincerely hope this does not offend anyone.

How to Use This Book

Lessons for the Stage is comprised of two courses, one introductory and one advanced, and chapters on scene study and exercising which are basic to both. Each course is sequential, and the second assumes a knowledge of the skills in the first, although these are reviewed and expounded upon in the second course. The Introductory Course, however, calls for no prerequisites other than being alive! The exercises included are valuable for anyone; neither a formal interest in drama by the students nor a formal degree in the teaching of drama is necessary or required. Self-awareness, awareness of the external world, and the ability to work independently and with others are all central to this course. Being able to present oneself and to perceive others in varied situations—action and interaction—are basic to drama and to any form of social life. What is being taught is not "enrichment" but the fundamental essence of education.

I have included a running commentary of helpful information for teacher preparation for the lessons in both courses. The commentary includes explicit directions, insights, further examples, warnings about particularly tricky spots in the lessons, resource material, and sources for many lessons.

I have tried to create this book so that it can be useful to acting teachers in any situation. Often a teacher has one class comprised of students at various stages of development, or teaches classes at both the middle school and the high school. Often the teacher may not even have a formal in-school course, but rather an after-school club or extracurricular activity. The material presented in this book, I feel, may easily be applied in all cases.

At a quick glance, a teacher may ask how thirty or so lessons will suffice for a semester or full-year course. The fact is that these are not daily plans; while many are designed to fill only a day or two, the performance assignments—such as the Newspaper or Painting exercises—will obviously take several class meetings for the entire class to complete.

Another important note in working with this book is that the theater games found in the Introductory Course may be used as ideal warm-ups—or, in fact, entire classes—in either of the two courses. Students enjoy playing certain theater games over and over.

While interest and variety are built into the acting class due to its very visual nature, staggering the daily plans will increase student enthusiasm. By this I mean that two performance assignments may run concurrently, with a typical weekly plan looking as follows:

Monday	Tuesday	Wednesday	Thursday	Friday
Presentation of "Painting" assignment	Presentation of "Dialogue" assignment	Lesson	Lesson	Scenework
Individual student performances followed by class and teacher critiques	Students perform in pairs followed by class and teacher critiques	Teacher-led instruction	Teacher-led instruction	Students work as independent groups; teacher travels to each to provide individual attention

Some teachers would rather do all of one type of performance assignment first, followed by presentations of a second type, third, and so forth. This kind of planning is obviously just as valid. The decision of whether to choose one of the above proposed plans, or even invent a third, is determined by many factors, including length of the individual class as well as the length of the course (i.e., semester, full year, quarter), class size, attitude, composition, and level of sophistication. Ultimately it is the teacher's decision. The only necessity, no matter which plan is chosen, is the individualized instruction and training of each student in the class. As Linda Loman in *Death of a Salesman* says, "Attention must be paid." So we must use whatever method is most effective in providing the best instruction to our students.

Part I
Introduction to Acting

Photo: Peter Boppert

The Miracle Worker by William Gibson

Introduction to Acting

The Introductory Course is just that—a beginning. Students develop an awareness of what it takes to be an actor: They learn the importance of attaining believability and truthfulness on stage; they are exposed to improvisational work, theater games, and exercises; they explore ways of creating characters; they become familiar with areas of the stage, body positions, and blocking notation; and, as a final project, they perform a scene from a play.

In another sense, this course reaches far outside the specialized field of acting. It teaches "life skills" as well, and so has a very wide potential appeal. This is a course which teaches trust and camaraderie, celebrates our differences, serves as a beginning in our growth to self-awareness, and promotes the sharing of ideas, concerns, opinions, and problems. These, and the elements mentioned above, are expanded upon during the Advanced Course, but the "seeds," if you will, are planted here. Therefore the Introductory Course takes on extraordinary significance.

Once again I would like to remind you that the twenty-nine lessons that comprise this course are not to be confused with daily plans, for most of these lessons may require several days to complete. I feel it is important to be disciplined, yet flexible, in following this guide. I also feel you should use it in a way most beneficial to you; one that allows you to see and encourage the richness and individuality of each student enrolled. Every student is special and can contribute to the class in a unique way. Enjoy!

Lesson 1
The Apology Lesson

Commentary

This lesson is a splendid one with which to begin an acting course. The Apology Lesson immediately engages student actors in an activity—and one which nearly guarantees success since there are no "wrong" ways for student actors to respond if the simple directions are followed.

The first day of an acting class, while exciting, can also be intimidating for many students. They are not quite sure what this course is about and what is expected of them. Needless to say, they do not want to be embarrassed in front of their peers. I have found that once the initial phone conversationalists ("Procedure," Part II) are selected, interest soars—and continues to do so throughout the remainder of the class. Volunteers become plentiful. The students enjoy the humor and are often astounded at the concentration and occasional bursts of emotion displayed by their classmates.

The discussion section of the lesson makes the somewhat foreign concept of the theater process—that is, the journey from playwriting to performance—seem understandable to these beginning students, for nearly every component of theater can be found in this exercise.

The Apology Lesson appeared many years ago in an instructional brochure distributed by the American Shakespeare Theater in Stratford, Connecticut, to which I am indebted for this wonderful method of initiating students into the world of acting.

Materials:

paper, pencils   some furniture
two telephones   (a table, chairs, etc.)

Procedure:

Part I:
Introduce students to the course. Tell them about the kinds of things they will be doing:

- improvisations
- theater games
- working on a scene from a play
- assignments aimed at developing an awareness of what
  it takes to be an actor

4

Also explain what the goals of the course are:

- increasing an awareness of self
- becoming more comfortable in front of a group
- developing poise and confidence
- learning basic acting skills

Ask students if any have seen a play. How did they like it? How does it compare to the movies or TV?

Part II:

Tell the students that we are going to do an exercise that will give them a better picture of what theater is all about.

Ask students to write an apology. This apology may be to a real or imaginary person. It can be an apology for something that really happened or it can be fictional. The only requirement is that it be an apology for a specific thing (not "I'm sorry for doing that," but rather "I'm sorry for blaming you when you were late for the movie").

Give students enough time to finish the writing. Ask them to read the apologies aloud. Commend all of them (it's difficult not to do this writing correctly) but praise the more believable ones.

Next, extend the written apology to an apology by telephone. Place two chairs back-to-back and have two telephones for the students to use. One person will use his written apology for the subject matter of the phone call. Encourage a dialogue. If the apology is readily accepted, ask one student *not* to accept the apology. This will lead to the idea of conflict as a necessary component in drama. (For a more advanced discussion about conflict, see the Commentary for Lesson 21.)

The next step in the lesson is to extend it to a face-to-face confrontation. Arrange the chairs as a sofa, easy chair, etc. Use a small table if you have one. Ask one student to come to the home of another to apologize. A third student may be added to the scene if needed to help move the story along.

In discussing the lesson with the students, make them aware of the fact that we began with writing on a piece of paper—just as a playwright does. Ask them what we added. How did we develop the piece? They should note the addition of props, characters, dialogue between two people, scenery, conflict.

Objectives:

The student will:

- learn the goals of the course

- become aware of the course outline
- use writing skills
- use creative imagination
- learn some of the elements of theater
- use body and voice to create character
- begin to understand the nature of conflict
- interact cooperatively with others
- accept ideas of other classmates
- improvise a fictional situation

Lesson 2

Actions: The Foundation of Our Work

Commentary

I think a percentage of actors on all levels are attracted to the theater for the glamour. Beginners are quick to say, "Give me a juicy scene and let me act!" without realizing that the moment to which they aspire comes only after years of rigorous training and commitment. While we should always appreciate their enthusiasm to play scenes of passion and grief and jealousy, we must guide them through the steps which eventually will equip them with the tools and sophistication necessary to play those moments with honesty and truth.

The place to begin our training is with the simple action: doing something. The word *action* has many shades of meaning as the study of acting progresses, with any given level of understanding and application based upon a previous one. Eventually we will learn that action—in all its connotations—unifies all aspects of the production work from performance to design. For now, however, let's keep it simple. An action, then, is the believable performance of an activity. It must be imbued with truth, beginning with a need to perform that activity (justification or motivation; see Lesson 3), and the performance itself aimed at achieving a desired result (objective or goal). If an action is performed truthfully, it will reflect concentration and attention to detail. The actor will perform it with commitment, and focus on making it real for himself rather than entertaining an audience, as is often the case with beginners. Also, it will not be done in an exaggerated manner—stemming from insecurities—with the actor "spelling out" what he is doing.

Perhaps this is a new concept for students of acting—that the emphasis is on process now and not on product. Another new and greatly appreciated concept is that all methods of performing an action are fine as long as they are truthful to the actor.

A variation of Part III of this lesson can be a lot of fun. Give the student actor one minute (timed) to make the item as many objects as possible without regard to size. In other words, a broom can become a toothbrush! Let the student's imagination run wild. It is a good "cooling down" exercise and, in a unique way, reinforces believability by demonstrating its opposite.

Materials:

a paintbrush	a pillow
a yardstick	index cards

Procedure:
This lesson will focus on the completion of simple activities performed in a believable way. Students will be encouraged to perform in a way that is unique to each, that reflects his own way of doing something. The lesson illustrates that student performances are not "wrong" but rather "different." Hopefully, this will encourage students to volunteer and test their creativity because they know they cannot be embarrassed by an "incorrect" response.

Part I:
Introduce the concept of *actions* in drama. They need to be performed as realistically as possible.

Define an area to represent a running brook in which there are several large rocks. Tell the students that we will all have to cross the brook by jumping from rock to rock. Discuss things to be aware of by asking them: Has anyone ever really done this? What do we have to think about *before* we perform this?

Responses should include the size of the rocks, their stability, whether they are sharp, slippery, etc. What happens if we slip off? How deep is the water? Is it cold? Is there anything in the water, etc.?

Have the entire class perform this activity. It is good to get everyone involved.

Do the same large-group activity for wading in the water by the beach, playing a game of volleyball, or hiking through the woods.

Part II:
Call students individually in front of the class to perform a simple activity lettered on an index card. The class should guess what each student is doing.

The cards include:
• packing a suitcase
• shoveling snow
• baking a cake
• making a sandwich
• raking leaves
• driving a car
• sewing with a needle and thread
• smoking a cigarette (how do you do it believably if you've never done it before?)
• working on a puzzle
• working on a model plane or boat
• painting a wall
• drawing a portrait

Again, discussion about each is important. Ask who has really done this. Encourage students to do each activity in a unique way— their own way.

Part III:
Bring the pillow, yardstick, or paintbrush to the center of the space. Ask the class what else the selected item might represent (the pillow could be a watermelon, a baby, a vase, etc.).

Ask students to come forward and endow the item with attributes of another object. Consider the object's size, weight, texture, value, etc.

Objectives:
The student will:
- develop self-awareness
- use creative imagination
- use his body in space
- become aware of aesthetic weight, size, texture, value, etc. of imaginary objects
- analyze behavior and activities of others
- realize that there are many ways to achieve a goal
- gain self-esteem

Lesson 3
Actions: Motivation

Commentary

The concept of motivation takes the study of actions a bit further because the actor must now add a degree of interpretation to his work. He no longer is interested in only *what* he is doing, but *why* he is doing it.

One way to begin the discussion after a student performs an action from the Motivation Worksheet is to ask the class what was seen, or what it thinks was the selected action from the given list. This is objective and provides immediate feedback to the actor, who will know if he has succeeded in communicating his task or action. If he has not, or if the class has difficulty identifying the action, the "why" becomes relatively unimportant. Encourage the class to offer suggestions for other methods of performing the task before discussing its motivations.

Sometimes it is interesting to ask various students (or even the same one) to perform the same activity with many different motivations. The complexion of the entire action will change, providing a valuable lesson for the class.

Materials:

Motivation Worksheet (following this lesson)

Procedure:

Today's lesson deals with Motivation.

Part I:

Begin the class by asking the students to think about the sentence "Close the door." Think about *who* you would say this to, and *why*.

After giving the class a moment to think about this, ask each member to say just those three words, "Close the door," keeping in mind the "who" and the "why."

Think about the different volumes used, the different tones. Ask the class why each response sounded so different from the others. The answers should lead you to discuss the nature of motivation onstage, that characters (and actors) must have reasons for everything they say and do.

Ask someone to stand on a chair, but before he does so he must justify why he is performing this action. Have the class guess what the motivation is. Ask each member of the class to give a reason, aloud, for standing on a chair.

Part II:
Pass out the Motivation Worksheets. Read the directions aloud to the class, and ask each student to select one of the actions and perform it with a specific motivation in mind.

Objectives:
The student will:
- learn the nature of motivation onstage
- use body and voice to justify actions
- be observant and constructively critique the work of fellow actors

Motivation Worksheet

Select a reason for performing one of the following actions. Perform it believably and with intent, or motivation. Remember that every action on the stage must be motivated. Use your imagination to create unique and original work!

cleaning your room

preparing a meal

sitting on a table

taking a photograph

holding an object over your head

putting up a tent

running up and down the street

closing a window

cutting up a piece of cloth

boring a hole in a piece of wood

weighing an object in each hand

balling up newspaper

combing your hair

writing a letter

not answering the phone

knocking on a wall

making a paper airplane

walking a dog

sitting alone on a bench

waving an umbrella

carrying flowers

standing on one leg

pouring water in a pot

hiding in a closet

Lesson 4

Detailed Actions and Gestures

Commentary

Our continuing study of actions emphasizes their importance for all stage work. They represent a "common denominator," for they figure heavily into all aspects of production—from acting and its complex components to design. They are also the only outward manifestation of characterization and motivation, as well as of sensory awareness, subtext, and emotional recall in future lessons.

Thus far we have progressed from the performance of the simple action for its own sake to the performance of a simple action in order to fulfill a certain objective. Part I of Lesson 4 develops our study further by allowing *character*—someone *other* than the actor—to "color" the manner in which the action is carried out. Part I examines the simple act of walking as it is executed by various people in various situations. After all of the student actors have performed, you may want to allow them to create their own reasons for unique walks and demonstrate these to the class. This encourages student-initiated, as well as teacher-initiated, activity.

In Part II, the Action Worksheet will call for the actors to create a series of actions in order to communicate both the "feeling" listed and the circumstances. Again, when the class discusses the actor's work, begin with the objective "what" (What did you see? What was the character doing?) before tackling the "why."

Materials:

Action Worksheet (following this lesson)

Procedure:

Review the use of details with the class. We have already worked on the details of simple actions. Today we will take the concept of detailed actions and gestures into two other areas.

Part I:

The first focuses on *walking.*

Begin by asking the class what "body language" means. Discuss the messages that people send through the use of their bodies both intentionally and unintentionally. Cite examples of this. Often the class will think of some also.

People also send these intentional or unintentional messages through the way they walk. Tell the class you will call volunteers up and quietly give each a circumstance which involves a walk. The class must guess, at the completion of the activity, what or who the person was. Examples are:

- the owner of a store is on his way to deposit a large sum of money in the night vault of a neighborhood bank

- a woman just selected as Miss America walks past admirers and photographers

- a teenage boy wants the girls to look at and admire him

- a law student walks to class after staying up all night studying for the bar exam

- a vacationer walks on the hot sand of the beach

- a homeless person goes to claim his recent inheritance, making him very wealthy

- a thief hides a gift under his jacket

- someone hoping for a job is late for his interview

- an old person is carrying heavy groceries

- a dancer takes the first steps after surgery

- a wealthy person walks his dog in the middle of a snowstorm

Part II:

Just as specific walks gave us information about circumstances, specific actions tell us what the emotional state or feelings of any particular character might be.

We cannot "play" these states of being. They are intangible, invisible. Rather, we must play specific actions that will evoke the feeling.

Give out the Action Worksheet. Go over it with the students. Tell them that they must create a set of circumstances that can be broken down into specific actions. These actions will communicate the "affect," or feeling. Tell them to play the entire story, not just a few actions. For example, "violence" is not just picking up a chair and threatening someone with it. Instead, enter the scene as if you are coming out of a store and you see someone slashing your tires. Then approach and play full action, bringing the scene to a conclusion.

Objectives:

The student will:

- continue to focus on specific details
- use the body to communicate specific attitudes and circumstances
- use creative imagination
- evoke feelings through actions
- work cooperatively

Action Worksheet

After selecting one of the following words, create a circumstance, or a series of actions, which evokes that feeling. (For example, after leaving a movie, you find that your car has a flat tire. Fixing it in the rain can make you irritable.) Remember that feelings are intangible. Your only method of creating the desired feeling is to play the actions within a given set of circumstances. The actions will produce the feeling.

conceited	hungry	depressed
brave	freezing	tired
intellectual	excited	joyous
victorious	frightened	vindictive
elated	timid	stunned
stressed	critical	claustrophobic
angry	successful	sensitive
		anxious

Lessons 5–8
Using the Senses

Commentary

Lessons 5–8 add sensory awareness to the actor's accumulation of skills. I say "awareness" because the actor has been using the senses already, but being aware of their effect on the actor helps to sensitize him to his environment. This enables him to more vividly and truthfully present his work to the audience. Ask the actors to talk about how the various tastes, smells, sounds, sights, and touches make them feel. Remember, there are no "wrongs"; these are highly individual responses which, in turn, produce unique actions on the stage and help eliminate stereotypical sensory responses (e.g., crossing the arms and chattering when the actor is cold). An added benefit of sensory work is that diverse responses foster an awareness of the actor's sense of self, the specific qualities that make him different from everyone else become apparent naturally.

Stress detail once again, this time as it pertains to the senses and the subsequent performance of actions. For example, in the "Delicatessen Exercise" in Lesson 5, Part II, how is biting into an apple different from biting into a piece of hard bread? How much chewing occurs before swallowing? How much resistance to the knife is there when you cut a piece of cheese? What smells most pungent? Is there sawdust on the floor, as in the old New York delis? Is there a bell over the door that rings as you enter?

In Lesson 6, Part I, ask the class what sensory details were most effective in the actor's performance. Part II is a group improvisation. Until now we have only performed individually. I have found that student actors adapt to group improvisations very quickly. Do not hesitate to guide the improvisation by stopping it, offering suggestions, asking questions, etc. Students find these exercises entertaining and really enjoy them. You may want to spend some time defining the word *improvisation,* although a more in-depth study will occur later in this course.

Lesson 7 will require the use of a prepared tape of sound effects and will call for the creation of an improvisation according to a series of steps. It may prove enlightening to the teacher that these steps— supplying the "who," "what," "where," "when," and "why" factors—are the very elements of much problem-solving activity, a necessary skill for journalism, social activity, detection, and a host of other fields.

Although the process begins with the sense of hearing, it is important to tell the students that the senses work together to produce an effect. For example, a blindfolded person who is not allowed to smell the onion he bites might very well confuse it with an apple. Such "confusion" often occurs in Lesson 8, when students bring "tastes" and "smells" to class and blindfolded classmates attempt to guess the object.

Lesson 8 is a lot of fun. The "disguised" tastes and smells are shared (requiring a number of plastic spoons and napkins). This is the most sensory of these lessons because the objects actually cause physiological changes, such as salivation, in the participants. When the tastes and smells are administered, it is important to tell students not to "broadcast" their approval or disapproval by making sounds, as these "comments" set up expectations for the blindfolded class members awaiting their turn. In discussing this with the class, the point may be made that these communicative sounds are similar to facial expressions, movements, stances, body language, etc., all of which help the actor communicate to the audience. Some of this has already been discussed in the lessons on simple actions. It may be concluded, then, that while we learn sequentially, acting is also a process of integrating all of these skills, techniques, and insights.

Lesson 5
The Five Senses

Materials:
can be done with none, although the teacher may want to provide some furniture pieces

Procedure:
This lesson will continue to deal with simple activities and will introduce the concept of the five senses. An awareness of the senses helps the actor grow as well as increases concentration skills and stimulates imagination.

Part I:
Review with students the idea that our lessons thus far have been concerned with believability because acting must be believable! We have performed numerous simple activities, paying great attention to detail as a way of creating that believability. Of course, the way we learn what details to use comes from our own experiences or from our observations of others. So much of learning to act comes from observation. We observe people, animals, plants, and inanimate objects for the purpose of using specific qualities they have for creating characters. Just about all of this observation is done through the senses.

Ask the class to identify the senses. You may then want to ask for favorite tastes, for the most disliked taste. Repeat with smell, sight, sound, and touch.

Part II:
Define an area of the space to serve as a perfume counter in a local department store. Tell the students that there are three types of perfume for sale: *April Showers, Midnight Madness,* and *Will He or Won't He?* Ask the students what they think the fragrance of each would smell like according to the name of the perfume.

Ask students to go into the store and "smell" the three kinds. Each student should decide on one kind to purchase. The class then guesses which perfume was purchased based upon the actor's reaction to it.

Define an area of the space to serve as a delicatessen. Have the class suggest the various kinds of foods available (salads, cold cuts, pickles, breads, cheeses, etc.). Ask a student to walk into the delicatessen and help himself to something to eat. The class should then determine, according to the senses used, what the choice was. Tell the actor(s) that the pantomime should be as detailed as possible.

Part III:

This part of the lesson will be an improvisation using four actors. Select the actors and tell them that they have rowed a boat to an island to have a picnic. Ask them what they have brought with them that would force them to use all five senses. Have them "act out" their picnic. Encourage detailed pantomime of eating, turning on the radio, spreading the blanket, and any other activity they choose to do. Encourage conversation also.

Tell the students at one point in the improvisation that it is getting chilly, that the sky is turning dark, and that it is beginning to rain.

When they get back to their boat, tell the students that the boat is gone; it was not tied properly and it has drifted away. What should they do? Ask them to act out a conclusion.

Objectives:

The student will:
- become conscious of the use of the five senses in acting
- understand the importance of the senses in acting
- use the creative imagination
- perform detailed pantomime
- interact cooperatively with others
- learn problem-solving
- communicate through facial expressions, voice, and body movement

Lesson 6
Sense Memory Exercises

Materials:
furniture for improvisational performances

Procedure:
This lesson continues work with the five senses or sense memory.

Part I:
Review with students the importance of using the senses in acting. Today we will begin with individual performances using the senses.

In responding to these performances, the actor must evaluate himself in terms of his truthfulness to himself. The class evaluates in a constructive manner, dealing with the actor's believability.

Improvisation 1: The actor walks into a movie house. He must smell the environment, see the people, hear talking. Perhaps he can feel the sticky gum on the floor. He should eat candy or popcorn and soda.

Improvisation 2: A person is in a flower shop and must touch and smell various flowers before purchasing some.

Improvisation 3: A person comes out of a cabin located high in the mountains. It is early morning. Smell the air; see a mountain peak in the distance shining in the sun. The sight is beautiful.

Part II:
This improvisation is for more than one person.

Improvisation: Two secretaries work in the payroll office of a large corporation. While they were out on their coffee break, a sudden rainstorm and the accompanying high winds have swept through an open window, disrupting the already filled-out and alphabetized paychecks. The checks are on the floor. Some are totally destroyed and all are in disorder and disarray. Now additional students may be sent in, one at a time, to ask for (or demand) their paychecks. You may want to extend this improvisation and send in the manager of the division or the company president.

You may need to ask the class for suggestions about how to end this improvisation. Explore the options, decide on one, and ask the actors to bring the scene to a conclusion.

Lesson 7

The Sense of Sound

Materials:

a tape of sound effects   paper, pencils, or pens
simple furniture pieces

Procedure:

Today's class will continue to explore the five senses, with particular emphasis on sound.

Part I:

Tell the students that today's lesson will focus on sound, and that, by themselves, sounds are often difficult to identify. Impress upon them that the senses work *together* for us.

Play a sound-effects tape. I make my own for this lesson. Sound-effects records are easily available at record/tape stores. Make sure that the tape you use contains a variety of sounds.

The tape should be divided into *places* and *objects*. The tape I made, for example, used the following:

Places: jungle, sailboat at sea, bullfight, bon voyage party at a dock, thunderstorm in the woods, aircraft carrier, railroad station, children in a playground

Objects: tiger roaring, car skidding and crashing, soldier drill march, music box, electronic effect, car horn

As you play the tape, students write down what they think the place is. After all of the places have been played, go over the results with them. Do the same for the objects.

Part II:

We will now "build" an improvisation around the sense of sound.

Ask the class to select one of the places on the tape as the environment of the improvisation. Ask for two actors who will supply the "who" of the improvisation. Ask the class to decide upon the relationship between the two characters.

Now we know the "who" and the "where." Ask the class to supply the "what"; that is, what is the situation? "When" is this scene occurring?

Now the improvisation begins. You may want to play the taped sound effect to provide some atmosphere, although it will only cover the first 45 seconds to a minute of the improvisation.

In evaluating the performance, ask the class if all elements of the story were covered—"who," "what," "where," "when," "why." Ask if the sound effect helped create atmosphere, and if the atmosphere was maintained after the effect stopped.

Objectives:

The student will:

- increase sensitivity to the sense of sound
- integrate the sense of sound into a story line
- construct an improvisation
- create a plot
- identify the elements of plot (who, what, where, when, why)
- work cooperatively with others
- use the body and voice to create characters
- problem-solve

Lesson 8

Working with Taste

Materials:
to be brought in by students in preparation for this assignment; one "taste" and one "smell" per student. These objects should not be identifiable by their outward appearance. Also, one spoon per student and paper towels.

Procedure:
Today's lesson will deal with sensory awareness.

Ask the students to sit in a circle on the floor. If the class is too excited as they enter, you may want to do a few relaxation exercises first.

Everyone has his respective tastes and smells with him, and these should be hidden from view. Explain the procedure of this exercise:

- Everyone in the circle will close his eyes while one student brings his taste to the center of the circle. It is important to inform students that there should be enough "taste" for everyone in the class.

- Everyone will have a clean spoon and a piece of paper towel.

- The person in the center will move to each member of the class, put a bit of the taste on that member's spoon, and "feed" the student.

- Everyone in the circle must keep his eyes closed until the person in the center has finished feeding the entire class.

Upon completion of this activity, students should *not* guess what the taste was but rather describe its attributes: texture, consistency, shape, size, etc. Was it sweet? sour? Did it change its texture or consistency once in the mouth?

Students may then guess what the taste was.

Another important rule is that students should not "comment" (a sound can be a comment) as they are fed, for this will set up expectations for those awaiting their turn.

After everyone has shared his taste with the class, talk about the exercise. Students may discuss the anxiety before being fed; they may note the need to trust each other; they may not be able to identify the taste of a familiar substance. Note the concentration with which they approached an activity they had always taken for granted.

Follow the same procedure with the smell.

Discussion should follow on the application of sensory awareness in acting.

Objectives:

The student will:
- become more aware of the sense of taste and its components
- become more aware of the sense of smell and its components
- trust his classmates
- learn the need for sensory awareness in acting

Lessons 9 and 10
The Environment and Its Effects

Commentary

The objective of Lessons 9 and 10 is to increase sensitivity to one's environment. Obviously this has its place on the stage, as actors must relate to the setting in any number of ways, from having lived in this environment all of one's life to visiting it for the first time. The first of the two lessons deals mainly with establishing the environment through detailed mime. In discussing an actor's performance for these exercises, you will undoubtedly need to address "indicating," or giving too much information. This involves exaggerated and often comical reactions to various environmental stimuli and is often due to the actor's insecurity about getting his point across. Actors often think that making the audience laugh is synonymous with success.

Lesson 10 deals with environmental effects on behavior, making us aware that some places make the character comfortable and others may cause him to feel ill at ease. (I thank Jerome Rockwood for the inspiration for this lesson.) These environmental elements affect how an action is performed, and authors use this idea often in charging a moment with emotion. A vivid example occurs in Dickens's *Great Expectations,* when Pip visits Miss Havisham in decaying Satis House. Here the abandoned, aging bride shows Pip the room where her wedding was to have taken place many years ago. The "great cake," now infested with mice and bugs, still rests on the table and cobwebs cover everything in the musty room. Another example is the children's fear of the Radley house in Harper Lee's *To Kill a Mockingbird*. The eerie darkness of the house, the overgrown weeds, the creaking swing on the porch, and the "poison tree" in the yard all work to produce a startling effect.

A discussion of environmental effects on emotion and behavior may include the role of the senses, thereby providing a transition from the previous lessons. For example, the sense of smell may evoke feelings of comfort or discomfort in such environments as the dentist's office, a library, a movie theater, an animal house at the zoo, or the botanical gardens. Another interesting point is that any given environment may have different effects on different people (Lesson 10, Part II). Generally speaking, how many "older" people enjoy loud, seemingly raucous tunes and the thronging crowds of a rock concert? Likewise (and again, generally speaking), how many "younger" people enjoy donning their finest clothing for Sunday brunch at an elegant restaurant, eating with polished silverware, and listening to a live quartet play classical music?

The study of environments is an important facet of training an actor. It is his acknowledgment of an appreciation for the effects that the environment has on his emotions and behavior that adds detail to his work while increasing his self-awareness.

Lesson 9
Creating Believable Environments

Materials:
none

Procedure:
Today's lesson will deal with environments.

Review the principles of performing simple activities and using the senses. When asking students what things they had to keep in mind, elicit responses such as "specificity" and "details."

The use of details will now be extended to include creating believable environments.

Tell the class that you will call upon someone to come before them and "create an environment" which you will privately choose. The class must then guess what environment is being illustrated.

The first environment is a zoo. After the first performance, deal with its details. What did the actor do to create the environment? What part of the zoo was being visited? What animal(s) is involved? Where was the actor's focus?

Ask another volunteer to do the zoo again. While not judging either, note the different choices made by the actors. You may want to lead the actors through the exercise again, noting details they should be aware of. As with all mime exercises, you may need to make the class aware of "indicating," or giving too much information (often through comical gestures) to the audience.

Other environments are:

- watching a sporting event
- a supermarket
- an elevator

Extend this activity by allowing students to select an environment of their own and act it out for the group.

There is much for the teacher to deal with during this lesson. Indicating is one important point, since beginning actors tend to do this a lot! Another is focus. Help students focus on specific areas of space, objects in the space which may be effectively used to help them reach their respective objectives, and attention to detail. This last element began with the simple activity in Lesson 2 and must continue throughout all acting training.

Objectives:

The student will:

- pay close attention to detail
- learn that detail creates an environment
- learn that indicating is not appropriate in acting
- use the body to create environments
- use creative imagination
- work cooperatively
- learn to focus

Lesson 10

Comfortable and Uncomfortable Environments

Materials:

possibly some furniture (chairs, tables, etc.) for improvisational performances.

Procedure:

Today's lesson will deal with specific factors in the environment that make us comfortable or uncomfortable.

Part I:

Begin by telling students that today's class will continue our work with environments. Today, however, we will take our study one step further and attempt to determine factors in an environment that make us comfortable or uncomfortable.

Ask for student volunteers to perform one or both of the following improvisations.

You may explain the plot of the improvisation to the entire class, or you may take the actors aside and tell them privately. The latter method often piques class interest.

Improvisation: A wealthy person is temporarily stranded in an impoverished and crime-ridden section of the city when his car runs out of gas. It is late at night and all stores are closed, except one all-night market, where the person hopes to be able to phone for help. The only other person in the store is unshaven and rather frightening to look at. The wealthy person is carrying a good deal of money and is not certain what to do.

Or

Improvisation: A student comes to his teacher's home for private tutoring. The teacher is upstairs, but calls down to the student to make himself at home. There are, however, materials on all of the chairs, leaving no place for the student to sit. These objects include such items as books (some of which are familiar to the student), the teacher's plan book, the teacher's grade book, the teacher's pet (a real one!). The student is uncertain where to sit, what he may remove from a chair, what he may touch, etc.

Ask the class to respond to the improvisation. What factors made the stranded driver and the student uncomfortable? What factors made the unshaven person and the teacher comfortable?

Ask the class, "Where do *you* feel most comfortable?" Answers will probably range from one's home or one's bedroom to the house of a best friend or relative. Then ask students to identify the environment that they feel least comfortable in. What are the factors that make people comfortable and uncomfortable?

Part II:

Choose two students to perform short improvisations in each of the following environments. One student is to be comfortable in the environment and one is to be uncomfortable. The class should be given approximately five to ten minutes to work on these prior to performance. After each improvisation, ask the class to identify factors in the environment that made the characters comfortable or not. The environments include:

- an art gallery
- a cave deep in the woods
- a sailboat
- a railroad station late at night
- an Egyptian pyramid

- a dentist's office
- a local bar
- a soup kitchen
- the principal's office
- the set of a popular TV program

Objectives:

The student will:
- learn improvisational procedures
- determine factors which make people comfortable or uncomfortable in environments
- pay closer attention to detail and increase observational powers
- create imaginary environments
- learn problem-solving

Lessons 11–13
Improvisation

Commentary

A. *You must understand. I don't feel this way. I'm only representing the townsfolk.*

B. *Yeah, of course.*

A. *You have to understand them. They don't like your kind around here.*

B. *Why?*

A. *Because . . . uh . . . well, you're different.*

These lines are from a shockingly real improvisation performed in one of my classes. Needless to say, the "different" ones had little difficulty in finding the right words to express their shock and indignation in the face of the unexpected situation. This improvisation became amazingly real, and any artificial posing and verbalizing quickly gave way to honest responses with emotion, facial expression, and body movement becoming excitingly alive and electrifying.

Improvisation is an important tool in the theater. It teaches all possible acting elements, from using the voice and the body to thinking spontaneously and adapting to the needs of the moment in an active way. For the acting teacher, improvisations instruct, clarify, exemplify; for the actor they are exciting and fun. Students love improvisation. It is a dynamic teaching method.

If you have had experience in improv work, you know that there are many ways to set up and conduct an improvisation. If not, follow the steps in the lesson carefully. It is important not to be afraid of stopping an improv if it wanders from the given subject and objective. You may need to get it back on track. After a while, you will become more familiar and flexible as you explore various kinds and purposes of improvisations. Allow students to create characters and situations freely. Let them stretch their imaginations.

Improv performances are followed by a discussion of the believability of actions and dialogue. Were the reactions to the situation justified? Through discussion, students learn that what is truthful to one character is not always so for another. Thus, individualization occurs and various human reactions to the same stimulus are arrived at. Often the discussion moves from the stage performance to personal reactions and experience. This is a wonderful aspect of improvs, as students see stage truth as a reflection of the world and themselves. A discussion of improvisation in general may include the fact that we all play a host of roles each day: the teacher, the dutiful child, the salesperson, the babysitter, etc. Improvisation is all around us!

Lesson 12 allows student actors to create their own circumstances based on the use of props. Stress that props must be integral to the action of the improv, not used merely as a decoration. This lesson focuses on environmental awareness, imagination, and modes of perception.

Lesson 13, Part I, defines the term *endowment*. Actually, students have been practicing this already (Lesson 2, Part III). Part II is a longer improvisation which requires two couples. It is important to end each of the first three segments when the respective objectives have been met. Also, know how long you want to devote to segment 4. Do not let the segments wander. The class discussion after this improvisation is often quite exciting, as students express their particular views on the subject, again extending the stage life to the everyday lives and viewpoints of the class members.

Lesson 11

The Purpose of and Sample Improvisations

Materials:
furniture for improvisational performances

Procedure:
This lesson focuses on improvisation. Part I will deal with its purposes and how to set one up. Part II contains sample improvisations. There are many! This lesson may serve for several classes, or you may want to do a few improvisations now and return to others at a later time in the course.

Part I: Purpose
Improvisation is one of the most useful tools in training an actor. When the actor is not confined to the playwright's words, his mind becomes a vibrant, creative script of its own.

Actors learn to develop a character, to note growth and changes in the character, to work for an objective or goal, to adapt to the needs of the moment, to think quickly and spontaneously, to overcome obstacles, to create meaningful dialogues, to be flexible and creative, to experiment.

There are many different procedures for setting up an improv. I have found the following steps successful:

1. Select actors to perform the roles (can be voluntary or selected by the teacher with a certain purpose in mind).

2. Tell the actors what the setting is, what the characters are generally like, what the conflict is, and what the goal is. Often this information is shared with the class at the same time, but it is sometimes appropriate for only the actors to know this information.

Contrary to some beliefs, improvs are not composed of idle rambling in both words and actions. Every word and action should be used to achieve the actor's objective.

3. Improvs end when the goals are achieved.

Some improvs must be "guided" by the teacher. Individual performers may require special help.

A well-performed improvisation can be wonderful. However, the class can learn just as much, if not more, when problems occur during performance. Post-improv discussions deal with problems in blocking and body positions, volume, and breaking character, as well as the "positives," such as reaching the objective, particularly good dialogue and/or characterizations, etc. Improvs serve as an excellent reinforcement for lessons on detailed actions, truthfulness on stage, justification, motivations, etc.

Part II:

Following is a list of suggested improvisations. The teacher should feel free to use the given improv situations as imaginatively and flexibly as possible. For example, the first one can be reversed so that the boy wants to play piano while his parents want him to play football. This also helps to define and build character.

Improvisation 1: A son must tell his parents that he would like to play on the football team when their dreams for him are to play the piano.

Improvisation 2: A popular student wants to copy the homework of another, who is new to the school. The latter wants to make friends at the new school, but feels it is unethical to allow anyone to copy his homework.

Improvisation 3: Two young women discuss one's choice to get married to a man she does not love rather than spend her life without a spouse. The friend feels people should marry for love.

Improvisation 4: A teacher has an opportunity to chaperone a trip to a foreign country for six months with a select group of students. It is a wonderful educational opportunity, but his wife does not want to go with him.

Improvisation 5: One friend confides in another that he was in on the theft of a VCR from a local store, although he did not actually commit the theft himself. He now feels guilty and asks his friend's advice.

Improvisation 6: A student makes an appointment with a teacher to discuss an important grade that was considerably lower than the student feels he deserves. The teacher feels the grade was appropriate. What resolution can be reached?

Improvisation 7: A young person goes to a school social worker to say that he sincerely feels that his single parent does not love him. The parent actually forgot the child's birthday and canceled a greatly anticipated trip to Boston. The child wants to move out. You may introduce a third actor in this improv, playing the role of the parent.

Improvisation 8: A woman starting a teaching career is unmarried and pregnant. She wants to give the baby to a caring couple, but wants to be able to keep contact with the child through visitation and letters. The couple does not like this arrangement. You may need to add a fourth person to this improv to act as a mediator (social worker, lawyer, adoption agency worker, etc.).

Improvisation 9: A young woman brings her fiance home to meet her parents. The parents are wealthy and frown upon the fact that the young man is "lower class." (This may also be done as an interracial or inter-religious situation.)

Improvisation 10: A daughter and her mother do not get along. After an argument, the daughter spends the rest of the weekend in her father's apartment on the other side of town, but does not tell her mother of her whereabouts to "punish" her. Now the three of them must decide on an appropriate action to remedy the situation.

Improvisation 11: A mother and father are waiting anxiously for their daughter's return. It is Friday night and they told her to be home by 11:30. It is now 1:30 A.M. They are obviously upset. She finally enters and must make some excuse for her lateness. (Actually, a student once played this and made no excuse! She merely told her parents that she thought a curfew was silly and she decided to ignore it!)

Improvisation 12: A young person comes to the home of his best friend at 2 A.M. The friend's parents are away for the weekend and he is alone. The young person says his alcoholic parents have beaten him and he has fled here for safety. What should they do?

Improvisation 13: After graduating from college, two friends are sharing an apartment and all expenses and bills as well. A has a responsible job and has come to resent the fact that B is not holding up his end of the bargain. B is a writer who, while not currently employed, lives with the expectation that his book will one day sell, and he will be able to pay A what he owes him. A, however, does not like the arrangement and wants to replace B with C, a friend who has just arrived in the city and has no place to live. The problem is that B refuses to leave.

Improvisation 14: Two girls are at home one Friday night. They are good friends, A and B. B has been asked to the prom by C, a young, handsome man. The girls are leafing through magazines for ideas for gowns, hairstyles, etc., when C enters and tells B he cannot take her to the prom. C must create a reason. During the course of the improv it is discovered that he has asked another girl to the prom.

Improvisation 15: Two friends enter a bar. One is of age but the other is underage. The bartender serves them. A police officer enters and questions the younger character's age. This character may or may not have a phoney ID. Allow the improv to develop on its own.

Improvisation 16: An employee is called into the boss's office for what he thinks is a commendation and a raise. However, the boss says that financial problems in the company have caused several cutbacks in the work force, and that the employee is being laid off. During this conversation the employee must convince his boss not to fire him.

Improvisation 17: One character is the owner of a small shop. The other owns the land that the shop is situated on. The latter has been approached to sell the land to make way for a new parking garage. The shop owner's goal is to convince the landowner not to sell.

Improvisation 18: The owner of a shoe store is concerned only with making money. He watches the work of his new clerk, an honest young person who does not believe in "forcing" people to buy shoes they do not like, or shoes that are old or have flaws. The clerk needs this job badly.

Improvisation 19: A girl is expecting the arrival of her cousin, whom she has not seen in several years. The cousin is supposed to be very proper and well-mannered, but is actually a "wild" young person looking constantly for a good time usually in the form of alcohol or drugs. The visiting cousin tells her hostess of her "need" and the hostess tries to talk her out of it.

Improvisation 20: A shy girl has been fixed up with a blind date. He suggests they use the girl's car (as he does not have one of his own) to go to dinner in a neighboring state. His real objective is to visit his girlfriend. The shy girl discovers this during the course of the conversation.

Improvisation 21: *The protagonist of this improv has been framed and sent to prison for a crime he did not commit. While there, he has become very friendly with his cellmate, a "leader" of the prisoners who tells the new prisoner that he knows and hates the men who framed the protagonist. The "leader" tries to persuade the protagonist to join his escape plan. The protagonist is afraid to attempt escaping but realizes that this may be his only chance for freedom and subsequent pardon.*

Improvisation 22: *Into town moves a family of "city people," one of whom is a brash, insensitive girl of 16. Finding himself in her class in school, a farm boy is surprised at her strange style of dress, her abrupt manner with the other members of the class, and her different dialect. One day, it is storming outside and the roads are in bad condition. Our boy is driving home from town and sees an overturned car. Upon examination, he finds the unconscious passenger to be the city girl. He decides to take her to his nearby home.*

Improvisation 23: *The manager of a traveling acting company is discussing a scene with one of his actors who is black, Jewish, or any minority. The mayor and two leading citizens of the town where the company is to perform come to welcome the group. Their real intention, however, is to deny the minority actor the right to perform. (While the reality of this situation occurring today seems remote, this improv is a good tool to introduce a discussion of discrimination.)*

Improvisation 24: *An army commander is imprisoned with his men. He is faced with the choice of seeing his men shot one by one or signing a false confession. The improv weighs duty against humanity.*

Improvisation 25: *A widowed woman (or man) 45 years old must tell her teenaged daughter that she is going to remarry. The "problem" is that the fiancé is 20 years old. The daughter is upset by the latter's age and tries to convince her parent not to go through with the marriage.*

Improvisation 26: *A teacher tells a student that he is resigning due to the pressures of his job, which have made him frustrated and upset. The student feels the teacher is very good one and attempts to convince him not to resign.*

Improvisation 27: *A girl is showing her new engagement ring to her friend. Soon the girl's fiancé enters. She thinks he is coming to set the date for the wedding, but in fact he is coming to take the ring back.*

Improvisation 28: *A woman thought to have died returns after three years to visit her sister. The latter had married the former's husband.*

Improvisation 29: *A girl has been blinded in a car accident. Her sister, with whom she has been sharing an apartment, wants her to move back to their parents, for she does not want to have to look after her.*

Improvisation 30: *A student has earned a partial scholarship to a private school. He has been summoned to the headmaster's office and expects to be suspended for low grades. The last thing he wants is to be suspended. His parents have very little money and he has taken an extra job at night to earn tuition. The parents will be sick at heart when they hear the news.*

Improvisation 31: *A very old and very rich man is dying in his hospital room. Suddenly, many of his "friends" and relatives visit. He has not seen these people for a very long time. They are all greedy and want to be in his will. Actors in this improv must form their own characters and ways to reach their objective.*

Improvisation 32: *(From Michael Gazzo's* A Hatful of Rain.*) Polo lives in a small apartment with his brother, Johnny, and his sister-in-law, Celia. Johnny neglects Celia and leaves her alone with Polo a great deal of the time. She recognizes their growing attachment and asks Polo to leave.*

Lesson 12
Improvisation and Props

Materials:
six props (I used a water pitcher, an empty coffee can, a large comb, a battery, a small vase of flowers, and a hand mirror)

Procedure:
This is a lesson in improvisation and props.

Discuss with the students the importance of props in a play. Ask them what a prop is and why they are important. Then show them the six props selected. (If the class is large, you can use more than six.)

Divide the class into two groups and have each group select half the props (in this case each group would have three). Each group must create an improvisation in which the props are an integral part of the plot. Use some examples if necessary to illustrate how props are important and not merely decoration.

Give each group approximately fifteen minutes to work on their improvisations. Then have the class regroup and present the improvs. The post-performance discussion should include why the props were important. Other areas of discussion may include the believability of the characterizations as well as the plot.

Objectives:
The student will:
- design a story with plot and characterizations
- integrete the props into the plot of the story
- create character through voice and body movement
- work cooperatively in a group situation
- share ideas with a large class

Lesson 13
Endowment

Materials:
an object which can represent a newborn baby (such as a rolled blanket)

Procedure:

Part I:
Hold the object in your arms as if it were a baby. Ask the class what it feels the object represents. They will know immediately.

Explain to the class the definition of *endowment,* giving the attributes of one object to another. Say, "I am endowing this blanket (or whatever object you choose to use) with characteristics or attributes of a baby. What are some of those attributes?" The class will deal with size, weight, aesthetics (one student said "fragile"), etc.

Ask a member of the class to hold the baby. Ask a member of the class who has actually held one to share with the rest of us the things we need to keep in mind when holding a baby.

Ask the person to give the baby to someone else. Change the conditions or circumstances. Perhaps the baby is crying, soiled, sick, dead (from Charles McGaw's *Acting Is Believing*).

Part II:
This activity has prepared us for an improvisation. Two sets of volunteers (one male and one female in each set) are needed.

The first set is told that it has a newborn baby, but that it is very poor and cannot afford to care for the baby. They have therefore decided to place the baby in the care of Couple B. They do so anonymously by putting the baby at the Bs' doorstep. There will probably be a good deal of discussion between the biological parents, but the end result is a "given." They must give up the child.

The second part of the improvisation concerns Couple B as it discovers the baby on its doorstep. The situation seems at first bizarre, but Mrs. B decides that she would like to keep the baby. Her goal is to convince her husband to agree with her.

The third part of the scene occurs when Couple A, two years later and financially secure, comes to the home of Couple B to retrieve its child.

After a while, stop the improvisation. Tell the remainder of the class that it must act as arbitrators in the situation. They may ask questions of both couples, and the actors must answer *in character*, justifying why each should be awarded the child.

After sufficient questioning, the class must decide who will be awarded the child.

After the improvisation is completed, allow the class to talk about the believability of the acting. They will probably want to discuss the ethics of the case as well.

Objectives:

The student will:
- learn the rules of improvisation
- use body and voice to create character
- share ideas in problem-solving

Lessons 14 and 15
Scene Study

Commentary

Scene study represents the practical application of all classroom theory, and as such, it is the most fundamental unit of any acting course. It is an important tool for the acting teacher and an important learning experience for the acting student. At this point it is important for you to go to Part III of this book, the Scene Study Unit, read the commentary, and become familiar with the various charts and study aids.

Now that you have examined the different facets of the unit, you can see that scene study includes literary analysis, character creation and development, blocking, set design, directing, vocalization, business, etc. As the majority of this unit is independent work, the project may seem strange and overwhelming to your students, who have been carefully guided by you to this point. They probably have no idea where to start. Assure the students that the guidance they rely upon will still be provided, that you will inform them of and lead them through the various phases of scene development. As your unit progresses, some students may truly enjoy the independence and need little, if any, help. Others will hound you.

I devote a certain number of periods per week to scene study (usually two), traveling from group to group, assisting, answering questions in some instances and asking them in others to help student actors make discoveries about the scene.

There is no set length of time in a scene study unit. I usually try to distribute scenes about three weeks into the course and give students approximately five to six weeks to work on them. This includes two class periods per week so that I can meet with each group. The first three weeks of the course, then, are spent trying to get to know the actors quickly, determining strengths and weaknesses that play an obvious role in scene selection. There are acting teachers who allow students to choose their own scenes and acting partners. While there are values to this method, I prefer to assign the scenes and the partners so that I can focus on specific individual needs, "stretch" the abilities of actors, or introduce certain actors to new kinds of material.

Students truly enjoy performing the scenes and watching their colleagues perform. As it is such a major project, you may want to schedule an evening—after all of the scenes have been performed and critiqued in class—when they can be performed for an audience. The event can be as large or small as you choose, from an all-school event to a department-only workshop to an invitation-only/parent and friend audience. Whichever you choose, I feel that there should be some acknowledgment of the successful completion of this work.

Lesson 15 provides an outline for the presentation of the scenes. Obviously Lessons 14 and 15 are separated by the length of the Scene Study Unit, some five or six weeks. However, I felt it would be beneficial for the teacher to view the lessons in close proximity to illustrate the relationship between them. Post-performance critique guidance is provided in the Scene Study Unit, Part III of this book.

Lesson 14
Performing a Scene

Materials:
pre-selected scenes
Scene Study Progress Charts (found in Part III of this book,
the Scene Study Unit)

Procedure:

Part I:
Inform students that a major project in this course is the performance of a scene from a play. Today you will give them a copy of the
scene you have selected for them. Students have also been assigned
partners.

Prior to giving out the scenes, inform the class that scene study
is exciting. It is the opportunity to explore another character, to
"get into his skin," perhaps to think about living in a different time
period and wearing clothes and exploring customs, gestures, and
manners that differ from your own.

Scene study, however, also brings with it a tremendous amount
of responsibility—to the scene, to your partner, to yourself. You
have to discipline yourself to learn your lines on time, bring in
necessary props and costumes, share ideas, trust your partner, etc.

Tell students that while there is a great deal of work ahead of
them, you understand that this kind of work may be very new to
them, and they may feel overwhelmed. Assure them that you will
work with each individual so that he may grow as an actor. Explain
that you will give lessons on blocking (you may need to define that
term) and help them create a schedule. Let them know, however,
that scene study is largely independent, and that independence
requires responsibility and discipline.

Explain the Scene Study Progress Chart. (Refer to Part III, Scene
Study, if necessary.)

Part II:
Pass out the scenes to the actors. Tell them that future class lessons
will deal with specific details about scene study, but today you
would like them to get acquainted with the scenes and their
partners. They should go with their partners to a comfortable and
private part of the theater to read the scene aloud. Explain that you
will travel to each group to answer any questions it may have.

Remind students that the Scene Study Progress Charts must be filled out for every rehearsal, including today. Give each group a copy. Collect them at the end of the period.

Objectives:
The student will:
- be made aware of expectations of the Scene Study unit in Part III
- become familiar with the pre-selected scene and partner

Lesson 15
Evaluating a Scene

Several classes will now be devoted to the performance of the scenes currently being worked on. Refer to Part III of this book, Scene Study, for procedure and post-performance critique sessions.

Materials:

actors for the scenes being presented will bring in their own props, costumes, etc. The class will need copies of the Scene Evaluation Sheet included in Part III, Scene Study.

Procedure:

As the actors prepare to perform, give the class the necessary information (name of scene, playwright, actors' and characters' names, etc.).

Tell the class to take brief notes on the back of the evaluation sheet during the scene—but not so many that they miss a substantial part of the performance!

The scene is performed and videotaped if desired.

At the completion of the scene, the actors discuss the Script Analysis Sheet, telling what the scene is about ("This is the story of what happens when . . ."), the characters' objectives, and the climax.

The next step is the Post-Performance Critique (see this section in Part III, Scene Study).

The instructor works with the actors to correct major acting problems in the scene. Depending on the actors, specific scene, and sophistication of the class, this process may take more than one class period.

The Scene Evaluation Sheets are completed as a homework assignment, handed in the next class, and given to the actors. This provides feedback from colleagues.

Objectives:

The student will:
- perform a scene from a play (including acting, creating set, costumes, props, etc.)
- with the class, critique the scene according to proper procedure
- analyze the scene from a literary/performance point of view
- correct acting problems through teacher coaching
- apply lesson to his own acting problems

Lessons 16 and 17

The Dialogue Exercise

Commentary

Some wonderfully imaginative work has resulted from the Dialogue Exercise. It is a great deal of fun while teaching an important skill—*justification*. I've placed it just after scene study has begun (Lessons 14 and 15) because it provides a transition from improvisational dialogue (Lessons 11–13) to memorized lines.

The Dialogue Exercise forces actors to create circumstances and actions to accompany the given dialogue. Each must justify the other. Depending on the size and experience of the class, you may ask the student actors to create one or two presentations. If you select the latter, you will need to consider the following: Should students create a performance for each of the given dialogues? Should students use the same dialogue for both performances? You might want to suggest that one presentation be a comedy and one a drama. This could lead to discussions of basic comedy and dramatic acting techniques as the presentations are performed.

When giving directions for this exercise, it is a good idea to create an example of what you expect. Perhaps the class as a whole could create an example before breaking up into pairs to invent their own. For this exercise, you may allow the students to choose their own partners.

Lesson 16
Justifying Dialogue

Materials:

Dialogue Sheet (following this lesson)

Procedure:

Part I:

So far this term we have worked with believable actions and simple activities, and we have also worked with some improvisational situations.

We will now deal with our first memorization lesson. Needless to say, it is a valuable first step in learning the lines for the scene work described in Lessons 14 and 15.

Hand out the Dialogue Sheets. Direct students' attention to the following points: There are two sets of dialogue; "A" and "B" represent characters.

Ask volunteers to read the dialogues aloud, and then give directions for the assignment.

Students should create one or two presentations using the dialogues on the sheet. If two, the teacher should decide whether both presentations should use the same dialogue, or whether each presentation should use a different dialogue.

The objective of the assignment is to create a situation in which the lines are justified, and which illustrates a clear relationship between them and the accompanying actions. The order of the lines cannot be altered, no words may be omitted or added, and Characters A and B must say their own "assigned" lines.

Students may also use costumes and props for their performances.

Ask if there are any questions. Set a performance date and tell the class that they may now work with a partner on selecting and practicing the dialogue.

Part II:

Let students disperse throughout the space with a partner (they may choose one) and work for a while. You may travel to each group to offer help.

Objectives:

The student will:

- continue to learn the necessity of justification
- memorize lines
- use the creative imagination
- use the body and voice to create characters
- make appropriate costume and prop choices

Dialogue Sheet

Dialogue 1

A: *What's that supposed to be?*
B: *Can't you guess?*
A: *I'm not sure.*
B: *You use it like this.*
A: *Oh, now it's clear.*
B: *Here, try it.*
A: *Hey, this is fun!*
B: *It never fails.*

Dialogue 2

A: *What are you doing?*
B: *You're kidding.*
A: *Can I help?*
B: *Well . . .*
A: *Please?*
B: *No, thanks.*
A: *Want some?*
B: *Not really.*
A: *Look at that.*
B: *I'm busy.*
A: *That's really amazing.*
B: *I know.*

Lesson 17
Performing a Dialogue

Materials:
to be determined by students in preparing for assignment

Procedure:
Today students will present the dialogue assignments they have been
working on.

Part I:
Tell the students that you will give them a few minutes to review
their performance. Allow each group to rehearse in a different area
of the space.

After a sufficient amount of time, reassemble the class.

Part II:
Students are now prepared to perform. Review the purpose of this
assignment: to make sure that every line is justified, and to understand the relationship between the lines and the accompanying
actions.

Ask one group to perform. After the performance, ask the class
for comments. Were the lines justified? Did they seem believable?
What was particularly good about the performance?

You may ask the group to perform again. This time, change the
circumstances and ask the class whether this change affects vocal
qualities or physical movement. Help students explore the possibilities of their brief dialogue. One of the advantages of this assignment is that it is brief enough so that line memorization is not a
problem. A host of "variables" may then be introduced which will
at once teach the class and stretch the performers.

Continue to select groups to perform.

Objectives:
The student will:
- perform rehearsed dialogue
- learn that all lines and actions must be justified
- use costumes, props, and a set for the performance
- learn the relationship between delivery of lines
  and other components of theater

Lessons 18, 19 and 20

Stage Areas, Blocking, and Stage Shorthand

Commentary

While most lessons in introductory courses are process-oriented and pertain to a growing sense of self-awareness, blocking and stage shorthand are technical skills necessary for performing scripted text. Look over the material carefully before teaching it in order to become familiar with the terminology, the strengths and weaknesses of stage areas, and body positions. The accompanying diagram will be helpful.

After imparting the basic information in Lesson 18, ask volunteers to use classmates in creating stage pictures where one actor is "stronger" than another due to stage area and body position. There are many other variables to consider when deciding upon "strength" or focus. We did not even touch upon levels—sitting, kneeling, standing on a stairway, etc.—space around an actor, contrast, and the elements of composition. Be aware that students may ask questions pertaining to these without using the "appropriate" terminology. You may want to augment this lesson to specifically address these other methods of attaining focus. I did not include them because of the introductory nature of this course. Instead, I refer you to the Dean/Carra book *Fundamentals of Play Directing*, which offers an excellent unit in this area.

Composition "rules" generally provide a norm which, when broken, tells the audience that something dramatic is happening. For example, three characters are conversing downright, when suddenly one quickly crosses upleft (a weaker stage area) and ends up full back (a very weak body position). The person crossing becomes the focus of the audience, which wants to know what has happened. Breaking the rules here denotes an important moment.

Lesson 19 deals with blocking notation and stage shorthand. Symbols other than the basic cross and denotation of character names are suggested. You may use variations of these or different ones if you wish. The point is to use the least amount of time and the smallest amount of space (since the directions are made in the margin of the text). Create a system that is understandable and immediately identifiable.

Lesson 20 is a wacky, fun-filled way to reinforce knowledge of stage areas and body positions. The three types of cards necessary for this game must be prepared in advance. Have fun!

Lesson 18

Stage Areas and Body Positions

Materials:
chalkboard and chalk

Procedure:
Today's class will be an introductory lesson on blocking.

Part I:

The class should sit in front of a chalkboard so that the teacher can draw diagrams during the lesson.

Draw a bird's-eye view of the stage and divide it in half horizontally:

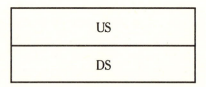

Explain that the half closest to the audience is called "downstage" and the half farthest from the audience is called "upstage."

Students are interested to know the derivation of those terms. Tell them that many of the earliest stages were "raked," so that the actors in the rear could be seen. "Upstage" came about because it was, indeed, "up" higher in the air, and "downstage" meant that the front of the playing area was "down" closer to the ground.

Draw another bird's-eye view of the stage and divide it in half vertically:

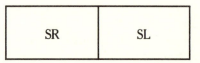

Label "stage right" and "stage left." If the class thinks you have mistakenly labeled the diagram, explain that stage directions are labeled from the actor's point of view.

At this point, you may bring your diagrams to life by actually walking to the areas of the stage and asking the class to name them aloud. You can also ask students to move to parts of the stage.

Draw a third bird's-eye view of the stage and divide it into nine areas. Ask the class to use their new knowledge of upstage, downstage, stage right and stage left in helping you label all nine areas. You may have to help them with the center corridor of names.

Upright	Upcenter	Upleft
Stage right	Center	Stage left
Down right	Down center	Down left

As you identify the areas, teach the students the abbreviations for them.

UR-#8	UC-#3	UL-#9
SR-#6	C-#2	SL-#7
DR-#4	DC = #1	DL-#5

Now you should ask the class to help determine relative strengths and weaknesses of stage areas. Ask what area of the stage is the "strongest"? Of course, you will need to identify "strongest" as that area which seems to take focus most easily, or that area to which the audience pays greatest attention.

They will probably say "downcenter." Lead them through all nine, assigning numbers to areas from strongest to weakest. The sequence should be:

DC, C, UC (explain that the center corridor is very strong),
DR, DL, SR, SL, UR, UL.

Explain that stage right is stronger than stage left because we read left to right. Our eyes, therefore, naturally follow stage right to stage left. Downstage is stronger than upstage (except, again, for the center corridor) because audiences will look at actors closer to them before those farther away.

Part II:

Stage areas have strengths and weaknesses when "all things are equal." Such a state, however, is rare since plays often have many characters on stage at once, and often they are all engaged in a variety of activities or a variety of body positions.

We will now talk about the eight standing body positions. Identify them as:

Full Front: The actor stands facing the audience directly
1/4 Right: half turn between full front and profile stage right
Profile Right: standing facing stage right
3/4 Right: half turn between profile right and full back
Full Back: standing facing upstage
3/4 Left: half turn between profile left and full back
Profile Left: standing facing stage left
1/4 Left: half turn between full front and profile left

Talk about the strengths and weaknesses of the respective body positions. Full front is obviously the strongest, with the quarter turns next, followed by profiles. Three-quarter turns can actually be weaker than full back. The full back position often has a sense of mystery associated with it that will bring focus to it.

Ask two students to move to certain stage areas and assume specific body positions. Illustrate how a stronger area may be made weaker when the actor in it is in a weaker body position than his counterpart in another area.

Part III:

Ask the entire class to move to the center of the stage. "Play" with their new knowledge by giving such directions as:
• all people wearing glasses move DR
• all people wearing anything red move UL
• anyone wearing sneakers move DL
• anyone wearing a ring move UC
  and so forth. It is a fun and active way to end class.

Objectives:
The student will:
  • learn the nine basic stage areas
  • learn the eight basic body positions

STAGE AREAS
and
BODY POSITIONS

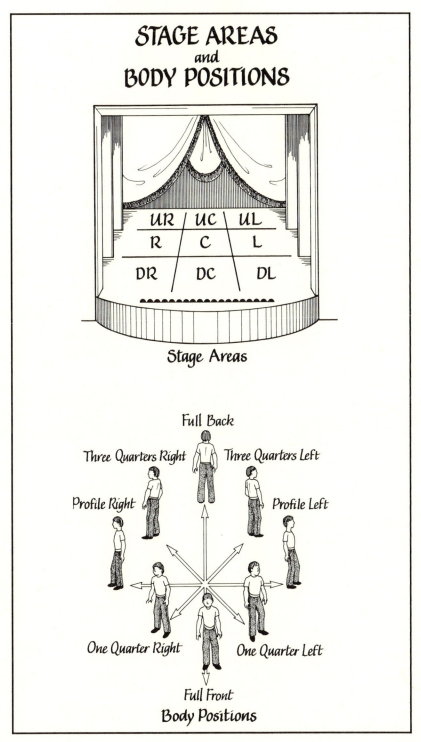

UR	UC	UL
R	C	L
DR	DC	DL

Stage Areas

Full Back

Three Quarters Right   Three Quarters Left

Profile Right   Profile Left

One Quarter Right   One Quarter Left

Full Front

Body Positions

Lesson 19
Blocking and Stage Shorthand

Materials:

chalkboard   paper

chalk   pencils

Procedure:

This lesson will deal with blocking, specifically stage shorthand.

Impress upon students the need for a reliable and quick method to take directions onstage. For this reason we use shorthand.

Students should be sitting near the chalkboard. Review with them the nine basic stage areas (Lesson 18) and the abbreviations for each. Review also the eight basic body positions and the abbreviations for each of these. These abbreviations are the first step toward learning stage shorthand.

Draw a basic set design on the board. You may want to use a design created by one of the groups in this class for their scene study. Tell the class that blocking cannot occur without a set.

Tell the class that they should imagine a character entering stage right and moving to the couch, which is located down center, and sitting on it. Write out the entire direction on the board. Tell them that writing down every direction in this manner is exceedingly tedious, not to mention the wasted time and energy.

Now write the direction using stage shorthand:

© ent. SR; x 2 couch DC; $

They will immediately notice the short amount of time needed.

Make a list of shorthand symbols on the board:

x = cross or move	$ = sit
ent = enter	$ = stand
© = Charles, or a character's name (always circled)	j = jump
	2 = to

Ask students if there are any questions. Dictate stage directions to the class and ask them to copy down the directions in stage shorthand. Ask some students to put these on the board. You may want to have students read the directions back to you. There are a variety of ways to do this.

Erase the board and draw a large page of text. Show students that shorthand is written in the margins of the text. Tell them that it is important to circle the word upon which the actor will begin the movement. This will add specificity to the blocking and guarantee that the actor will always move on the same word.

Explain that an actor finishes the cross with the end of the line. While this may sound mechanical or artificial, it is an important rule of the stage. Demonstrate this for the class, making it look realistic and natural.

Explain and demonstrate a direct cross and a curved cross. Ask the class when a curved cross may be used. Show the symbol for a curved cross.

$$\widehat{X}$$

Extension:

Extend the lesson by asking students to dictate stage directions to each other. Students should use stage shorthand in blocking their respective scenes.

Objectives:

The student will:

- learn stage shorthand
- learn the purpose of stage shorthand
- use stage shorthand to block scenes

Lesson 20
The Stage Directions Game

Materials:

Stage Directions Game
(must be made ahead of
time)

a stool
a ladder
a chair

Procedure:

As an introduction to this game, tell the class that they will have recently received their scenes for study and performance. As blocking is such a critical part of any performance, we will use today as a review of basic stage areas and body positions. You may want to review them at this point.

Stage Directions Game

The class is divided into two teams, A and B. A sends one of its members up to pick two cards, one from Pile 1 and one from Pile 2. Pile 1 has one specific part of the stage written on it. Pile 2 has a specific body position written on it.

The team member has fifteen seconds to go to the part of the stage designated and assume the body position designated.

The rest of Team A has twenty seconds to tell the part of stage and position.

If both the team member and the rest of the teammates are correct, Team A gets five points. It may also choose an Activity Card from Pile 3.

The team member who just "performed" has thirty seconds to mime the activity described on a card in Pile 3. The teammates have thirty seconds to identify the activity. If correct, the team gets ten points.

Team B now has a chance to score.

Items on cards in Pile 1: DR, SR, UR, DC, C, UC, DL, SL, UL.

Items on cards in Pile 2: (I used 24 cards because I have a large class. You may choose to use fewer):

Sit FF	Stand FB
Sit on stool 3/4 L	Stand 1/4 R

Sit 1/4 R	Sit 1/4 R
Sit prof. L	Stand prof. R
Kneel 1/4 R	Stand FF
Stand 1/4 L	Kneel FF
Stand on stool 3/4 R	Stand prof. R
Lie down with head SR	Lie down head DS, feet US
Stand on ladder prof. R	Kneel 1/4 R
Sit on chair 1/4 L	Lie down head US, feet DS
Sit on floor FF	Sit FF Indian style
Sit prof. L	Stand on one leg 3/4 L

Items on cards in Pile 3 (Activity Cards):

You are a caterpillar that turns into a butterfly.

You are an eagle swooping down to catch a squirrel.

You are writing with a pen twice your size.

You are an opera singer who gradually turns into a dog.

You are a wolf serenading the moon.

You are a bomb falling from a plane and exploding.

You are a cowboy riding a bucking bronco.

You are a rock singer.

You are a bird hatching from an egg.

You are an anteater scavenging for food.

You are a tight-rope walker who has to sneeze.

You are a bullfighter who would rather be a ballet dancer.

You are a three-way lightbulb in a lamp.

You are a high-fashion model whose skirt or pants has ripped.

You are a child whose lollipop weighs 50 pounds.

You are concrete being poured from a truck; when you harden you become a sidewalk.

You are a flag waving in the breeze.

You are a baby whose diaper is wet.

You are Dorothy from *The Wizard of Oz*.

You are trying on a new pair of shoes and they start dancing with you in them.

You are an alien.

You are a sergeant who has a giggling problem.

You are a sea monster who eats a ferry boat and its passenger.

You are a ballet dancer who stubs a toe while dancing.

Objectives:
The student will:
- learn the nine stage areas
- learn the eight body positions
- learn to think quickly
- communicate concepts through sounds and body movement/ gestures

Lesson 21
Objectives and Beats

Commentary

The enormous importance of objectives necessitates this special commentary. The objective—what the character wants ("motivation" is *why* he wants it)—is extremely important, as it propels him through the scene. It should be one of the first steps taken in scene analysis, as the actors begin to focus on just what this scene or play is about. Stanislavsky talks of the "super-objective"—the one overall goal a character wants to attain in a play. The smaller objectives of each scene must relate to, or fuse into, this larger goal.

Often one character's objective is to control or persuade another to do or say something. This can be realized in a variety of ways, from controlling through words—as in *Antigone*, where Creon and Antigone carry on a duel of philosophies—to controlling through blackmail— quite an intriguing and theatrical method, used by Lillian Hellman in *The Little Foxes* and Ibsen in *A Doll's House*—to controlling through action.

The most effective, theatrically speaking, is through action. We need only look at O'Neill's *Desire Under the Elms* to witness Abbie Putnam's terrifying means of controlling Eben: She proves her love is for him and not driven by a desire to own the much sought-after farm by murdering her child, the rightful heir to the farm. And Richard III obtains his objective of winning the English throne by killing all of those in line ahead of him.

Of course there are other means of attaining one's objective. Iago is the complete villain when he tricks Othello into believing that Desdemona is unfaithful to him; and Elmire uses flirtation to prove that Tartuffe is an imposter as her husband hides under a table to witness Elmire's accusations.

Taking this discussion of control one step further, I feel it is very closely related to the conflict of a scene or play. While we have always been taught that conflict is the clash of opposing forces, I propose to define it as the possibility of control. The Montagues and Capulets cannot "control" each other. Their time-worn hatred for each other prevents them from ever being friends or allies. But Romeo and Juliet transcend the differences between the two families so that a possibility of ending the turmoil—thus, controlling it—lies in their union. Another example is Jay Presson Allen's *The Prime of Miss Jean Brodie*, where the headmistress of a private girls' school has tried relentlessly for years to dismiss a teacher, Jean Brodie. Brodie, however, is seemingly invincible. A former student's testimony regarding Brodie's role in the death of a classmate enables the headmistress to exercise control, and she subsequently wins the conflict. The testimony makes Brodie vulnerable. I often refer to this vulnerability as "the chink in the character's armor," and actors would do well to determine where this lies—and then how to control by taking advantage of that vulnerability.

Obviously, the characters do not always reach their objectives. The obstacles may be too formidable. However, without a doubt, the greater the obstacle, the more interesting the scene or play. The obstacle to attaining one's objective makes the dimension of the character, and the passion and drive of a character to overcome the obstacle makes the dimension of the play.

The dialogue sheet used in Lesson 21 is an excerpt from a play entitled *Circles in the Sand,* by Jonathan Panagrossi, a talented playwriting student of mine. I am grateful to Jon for allowing me to use his work in this book.

Materials:
Dialogue Sheet from *Circles in the Sand* (following this lesson)
pencils
individual scenes being worked on in the Scene Study Unit

Procedure:

Part I:
You may begin class by asking if anyone knows the definition of an objective. An objective is something that a character wants to obtain in a given scene or play. For example, a character may want to win someone's friendship, or get another character to love him, or find a solution to a problem. The objective affects everything the character does in the scene, including vocal inflections, action, blocking, and business (small activities, such as washing dishes, putting on gloves, pouring a drink, combing one's hair, etc.).

Part II:
Pass out the Dialogue Sheets. Tell the class that a scene is made up of "beats," and we will use the text of the Dialogue Sheet to identify these divisions. Beats are the idea units that make up a scene. Each is concerned with a specific topic or bit of subject matter, and each beat relates directly to the overall subject of the scene.

Beats can, in a way, be compared to the paragraphs of a composition in that each paragraph relates to a certain idea. When the idea changes, a new paragraph is begun. Think of beats, then, as idea units.

Ask two volunteers to read the scene aloud.

After the completion of the reading, ask the class to draw a pencil line dividing the first and second beats. It should be after Brad says, "Sit down," and before he says, "Did you make up with Vic?" The idea clearly changes from discussing why Brad is sitting alone in the dark to Emily's relationship with Vic.

Give the class time to divide the rest of the scene into beats:

- Brad's line "So what's new?" initiates the beat about friendship.

- Brad's line "What did you call me?" begins the beat about Brad's name.

- Emily's line "You know, Brad, we have a lot in common" begins a beat dealing with the relationship between Brad and Emily.

Discuss the beat divisions and their purpose.

Actors often memorize a scene by beats, which prevents them from feeling overwhelmed by the overall amount of memorization.

Beats signal subtle changes in acting toward an objective. Beats contain minor intentions or objectives which feed into the major character objectives of the scene.

Ask what the overall scene objectives are for Brad and Emily. You may get a variety of answers. Some students may feel that Emily wanted to "win" Brad from the very beginning of the scene. Discuss some of the ways she attempts to do this in the various beats. Is Brad's objective to win Emily? Is it to enjoy the evening alone? Decide on their respective objectives and determine how each beat helps to attain that objective.

Objectives are important. Actors should never "wander" through a scene. Rather, everything they do or say must be aimed at attaining a specific goal.

Part III:
Students should meet with their respective scene partners to divide their scene into beats and determine character objectives.

Objectives:
The student will:
- learn the definition of objectives

- learn the definition of beats
- learn the importance of objectives and beats
- divide a scene into beats
- determine the character objectives for a scene
- divide his own scenes into beats
- determine character objectives for his own scenes

Dialogue Sheet

from *Circles in the Sand,* by Jon Panagrossi

It is night and everything is dark except a light on Brad sitting on the porch alone. Emily enters behind him through the door.

EMILY: Beautiful night, huh?

BRAD: *(Startled)* Yeah, it's all right. God, you gave me a heart attack. What are you up to? I thought you all went to sleep. It must be three-thirty now.

EMILY: I knew you didn't go to bed. Why are you up?

BRAD: I just . . . I couldn't sleep. You know. Actually, I just kinda came out here. I like to stay up sometimes. I love the dark and the beach, to listen to the waves and think about things. I guess that's weird, but . . .

EMILY: No.

BRAD: I just love the dark. When I was little, I used to be petrified of the dark. I was so scared. My parents wouldn't let me sleep with the light on, so I used to leave my door open and turn the hallway light on. Then I'd put the covers over my head and try to sleep. I guess it's ironic that now I love the dark. I just like to sit out here alone.

EMILY: Well, listen, I know what you mean. I'll leave you alone.

BRAD: No, you can stay. I'm not trying to get rid of you. Sit down. Did you make up with Vic?

EMILY: Yes. He's such a big jerk sometimes. And sometimes he's so sweet. Like when I came in he told me he loved me and he was sorry. I don't know. I can't figure him out.

BRAD: As long as you made up. So what's new?

EMILY: Not much. It's been fun up here so far, hasn't it? All of us here.

BRAD: Yeah.

EMILY: I mean, we're really lucky to all be here together. We're all like best friends, you know. Almost like a family. Not everyone is so lucky.

BRAD: Yeah.

EMILY: It's important, even if you have a lot of friends, to have a small group of close friends to fall back on.

BRAD: I know. You're right. Look at me, I have a few friends and everything, but . . .

EMILY: A few!

BRAD: Yeah, a few. I'm friends with a few people, and I still . . .

EMILY: How can you say a few people. Brad, you know everyone. Everyone is your friend. I couldn't name one person that doesn't like you. I cannot believe what I'm hearing from you, Bradley.

BRAD: What did you call me?

EMILY: I called you Bradley. That is your name, isn't it?

BRAD: Yes, but I think you're the only other person ever in my entire life to call me Bradley besides my mother! Even my father calls me Brad!

EMILY: I kind of like Bradley. It makes you seem much more intellectual and worldly.

BRAD: When I hear the name Bradley I can only think of a rich person's German Shepherd. *(With an English accent)* "Sir, there's an intruder on the grounds. Shall I sic Bradley on him?"

EMILY: *(Laughing)* That's not true at all. You know, Brad, we have a lot in common.

BRAD: What do you mean?

EMILY: I think the way we look at life is different than most other people, you know?

BRAD: I guess so.

EMILY: What makes you happy?

BRAD: What?

EMILY: What is the secret to happiness? It's hard to be happy sometimes. Like Vic . . .

BRAD: He's so simple in a lot of ways. He's arrogant and he's always involved in what everyone's doing, but he only really cares about himself.

EMILY: Sometimes I wonder about me and Vic. I mean, on one hand it's been so long and I love him so much—but the way he treats me. What do you think?

BRAD: I don't know.

EMILY: Brad, tell me something. Did you ever think about us?

BRAD: We're friends. We're like best friends.

EMILY: Nobody talks to me and cares about me like you do. Be honest. Did you ever think about it?

BRAD: I guess sometimes I get jealous of Victor. Only because of . . . I don't know.

EMILY: How do you feel about me?

BRAD: Are you gonna make me say this?

EMILY: Yes.

BRAD: I like you.

EMILY: And . . .

BRAD: I really like you a lot.

EMILY: I always think about what we would be like. I sometimes feel like, if I broke up with Victor, that . . . you know . . .

BRAD: This is weird, huh?

EMILY: Yes.

(After silence and staring at each other they kiss and the lights fade.)

Lesson 22

Theater Games

Commentary

Theater games are a great deal of fun. At the same time they teach student actors so much. While I have devoted Lesson 21 to these activities, feel free to use them at any time in the course. You may choose to do an entire unit with these games, or use them as "warm-ups" or "cool-downs" before and after other lessons.

Theater games and relatively new offshoots, such as "theater sports," have become increasingly popular. Variations of the "old standards" and totally new ones are created all the time. I am thankful to the many teachers and students who, through the years, have introduced me to the games included in this lesson.

The theater games are listed in two groups. Brief theater games, which last approximately ten minutes, are:

"Zoom"	"Alphabetizing"
"Concentration Now Beginning"	"No, You Didn't"
"Donkey, Rabbit"	"Object Toss"
"Circle Imitation"	"Changes"
"Freeze"	"Storytelling"

Longer theater games, which last an entire class period, are:

"Airport"	"Mirrors"
"To Tell the Truth"	"Chain Improvisation"

The procedure for each game can be found in the following pages. For theater games, the student will:

- learn to think quickly
- adapt to the needs of the moment
- improve listening skills
- work cooperatively with other students and the teacher
- follow directions
- use the body and voice to create characters and stories
- learn to use body language
- relate theater games to skills needed for acting
- improve concentration powers

Materials:
none

Brief Theater Games
"Zoom"

Procedure: The class sits in a circle and sequential numbers are given to each student clockwise.

> *Step 1:* When a number is called, that person says, "Who, me?" The person who called the number responds, "Yes, you." The person called continues, "Couldn't be." The caller says, "Then who?" The person called says another number, and the sequence begins again.

> *Step 2:* While the above dialogue is taking place, everyone in the circle gently slaps their knees or thighs, creating a definite beat or rhythm. One word is spoken on each beat.

> *Step 3:* Whoever is selected to begin the game says, "Zoom, zoom, zoom number " followed by the desired number. This is the only time "zoom" is mentioned.

> *Object of the game:* to be the one remaining after all other players are "out." A player is "out" if he forgets the dialogue, does not adhere to the beat or rhythm while speaking the dialogue, or calls out the number of a player already out.

"Concentration Now Beginning"

Procedure: This game is very similar to "Zoom." Students are still in a circle and, as with "Zoom," assigned a number. Students are taught the following physical activity:

> *Step 1:* slap your thighs once
> clap your hands once
> snap fingers on your right hand
> snap fingers on your left hand

> *Step 2:* A student whose number is called says his number when he snaps the fingers on his right hand; then he calls another number when he snaps the fingers on his left hand.

> *Step 3:* After this, the class continues to slap the thighs and clap the hands. The new number called then responds by saying his number on the right hand snap and choosing another new number on the left hand snap.

Step 4: Whoever is selected to begin the game says, "Concentration now beginning," one syllable on each beat created by the physical activity cited above. This is the only time that these words are spoken.

Object of the game: to be the one player remaining after all other players are "out." A player is out if he does not properly perform the activity described in Step 1 above, does not speak the dialogue on the corresponding part of the activity described in Step 2, or calls out a number of someone already "out."

"Donkey, Rabbit"

Procedure: The class stands in a circle, and the teacher stands inside the circle. The teacher says, "I'm going to point to someone and say the word, 'Donkey.' When I do, that person must stand at rigid attention by the time I count to ten."

Try several students, and speed up the counting.

Next, introduce "Rabbit." The person pointed to puts his forefinger on the nose; the students standing on both sides of that individual come over to him and put up two fingers near each ear. This should create a picture of a rabbit.

Do some Rabbits and mingle a few Donkeys to keep the students alert. Next, introduce "Elephant." The person pointed to makes two fists and places them together. He then places the two fists at the end of the nose to create an elephant's trunk. Again, students on either side of that individual come over and put up a hand with fingers spread to create the elephant's ears.

Now intersperse Elephant with Rabbit and Donkey.

Next, introduce "1776." The person pointed to holds the American flag; the person to his right holds and plays the fife; the person to the flag-holder's left plays the drum. The full trio should look like a Revolutionary War painting.

Again, intersperse 1776 with Elephant, Rabbit, and Donkey. The last animal to introduce is "Hippopotamus," which is created by the student swiveling his hips.

Try all five variations. There are many others, and if your class is enthusiastic about this game, allow them to create their own.

"Circle Imitation"

Procedure: Ask the entire group to stand in a circle, with plenty of space between each student. Ask one volunteer to go into the center of the circle and begin a "repeatable" movement. He should do the movement over and over as the rest of the class observes.

The student then begins to move toward any member of the circle, stops directly in front of that person, and repeats the movement as the chosen student tries to mimic in his place. When the initiator of the movement is satisfied that the "follower" has caught on, he takes that person's place in the circle and the "follower" continues the movement into the center of the circle. He or she then changes the movement to something entirely new, selects a new "follower," and repeats the above process. Continue until the entire class has had a chance. Sounds may be added to the movement also.

"Freeze"

Procedure: Ask two students to come up before the class. They can begin a scene about any topic they would like. The leader may have to give them suggestions or guide them to find a topic. At any point during the scene, a member of the class calls "Freeze" and takes the place of one of the performers. He or she then uses the frozen position that the remaining actor is in to initiate a new set of circumstances and hence a new scene. For example, in our class one student was teaching another a particular ballet step. They had their hands above their heads when a class member called "Freeze." He then replaced one of the dancers, stood on the opposite side of the stage, and pantomimed throwing a ball to the outstretched hands of the "former ballerina." This continues until all members of the class have had a chance to participate. After a while the freezes come more quickly and the students become more imaginative.

"Alphabetizing"

Procedure: Tell the students that you are going to time them as they do the following activities:

- alphabetize themselves by first name
- alphabetize themselves by last name
- spell their first names backwards and alphabetize themselves. A fun extension of this is to ask them to pronounce their first names backward. Most names take on an odd, sci-fi quality.

"Circle Impulse"

Procedure: Ask the class to stand in a circle and take hands. The teacher is on the outside of the circle. Tell them you will tap a student on the shoulder and that student should gently squeeze his right hand. When the person to his right feels the squeeze, he squeezes his right hand. The impulse continues around the circle until it comes back to the person who started it. That person calls "Time" and the teacher stops timing the event. Have the students try this several times until the time it takes for the impulse to return is diminished considerably.

Tell the students to close their eyes when you do it again. See if they can maintain the short amount of time.

"No, You Didn't"

Procedure: The teacher can demonstrate this game. Ask for a volunteer to sit in front of the class facing you. Instruct the student to say "No, you didn't" as many times as he wants as you tell a story. Each time you are interrupted you must change what you said when you were contradicted. For example:

TEACHER: Last night I went to the movies.

STUDENT: No, you didn't.

TEACHER: You're right. I went to the store. I bought some potato chips.

STUDENT: No, you didn't.

TEACHER: I bought some apples.

And so forth. The game makes the "teacher" or storyteller think quickly, as well as provides a great deal of humor and fun.

"Object Toss"

Procedure: Ask the class members to stand in a circle with you on the inside holding a soft, tossable object.

Tell the class that you will toss the object to a certain person in the circle. That person must immediately toss the object to the person to his right. The object keeps traveling until it returns to the person to whom you originally tossed it.

When tossing the object, you will direct that person to call out a specific number of words beginning with a letter of your choice. The goal of the game is for the person who receives the object from you to respond with the appropriate number of words before the object returns to him.

For example, toss the object to A and say, "Three words beginning with the letter 'C.'" That person must comply before the object returns to him or he is "out" and must leave the circle.

The leader should vary the number of words and change the initial letter every time he begins a round.

When there are only two players left, ask them to leave seven or eight feet between them. You may, at this point, need to limit the number of words starting with any particular letter to two or three.

"Changes"

Procedure: Have two students come before the class to demonstrate the game. One student studies the other's appearance. Then the person who has done the studying turns his back. The other student adjusts an article of clothing or makes any kind of change in appearance. The first student tries to guess the change.

Have the entire class stand in two lines facing each other. One student will study the student directly opposite. Begin with one change in appearance. Then move on to three changes. Have the students change partners at some point and try four changes.

"Storytelling"

Procedure: Students sit in a circle. One person begins to tell a story. He is encouraged to be as creative and imaginative as possible. After a given amount of time (either timed or arbitrarily decided upon by the teacher), he stops and the person to his right continues the same story, adding twists and imaginative details of his own. Continue in a like manner until all class members have had a chance. If the class is small, you may want to play two rounds of the game.

The next part of the game is to have each person say only one word in the telling of the story. Continue rapidly around the circle as these individual words form the sentences which comprise the story. Obviously, there will be many rounds to this session.

Ask the class members to choose a partner and tell a story one word at a time. Ask them to increase the speed, trying to create a natural flow of words in relating the story. You might ask each group to perform their story for the remainder of the class. Ask the class which of these two-member teams works best together.

"Airport"

Procedure: Set up two rows of chairs back-to-back in the center of the playing area to create a five-foot aisle.

Tell students that this aisle represents the runway of an airport. Choose two volunteers to act as the "airplane" and the "control tower," respectively. They stand at opposite ends of the runway facing each other. Tell the class that it is a particularly dark night, and electrical problems have broken communication from the plane to the control tower. However, the plane can still hear the control tower. To make matters worse, a terrible storm has made visibility quite bad, and it has also blown several objects into the runway.

To produce the poor visibility, blindfold the airplane. After that, put various objects (furniture, etc.) haphazardly throughout the runway (of course, it must be possible for the plane to get through the "obstacle course" without making contact).

It is the job of the control tower to direct the plane safely from one end of the runway to the other. If the plane should hit any obstacle, the game does not stop. Rather, the number of hits is counted, and the plane continues to the end of the runway.

When discussing the game, elicit from students the process of giving and taking directions which this game teaches. They will note that specific instructions, which use minute details, are better than general ones. Also, relate the game to theater: the runway is the play, the plane is the actor/character, the control tower is the director, and the obstacles are conflicts.

"Tell the Truth"

Procedure: Tell the class that we will play a theater game today that will test the student's ability to tell a fictional story as if it were true—and as if it had happened to him!

Divide students into groups of three or four, depending on the size of the class. The group will decide upon a "story" or event/experience that happened to one of them, and then tell it to the remainder of the class, using the pronoun "I" and relating the story as if it were an experience that happened to each of the group's members.

Each group will move to a private part of the space. Each member of the group will relate an experience that happened to him at some time. This experience should be somewhat capsulized. After all members have shared an event, the group decides upon one of these stories to tell the rest of the class. If they select A's story, A should re-tell it to his group *in detail*. Upon completion, the group should ask questions of A to clarify certain parts.

All groups reassemble, and one comes to the front of the playing space. One person in this group proceeds to tell the story as if it were his story. At some point, the teacher says "Stop" and the next group member continues the story, now telling it as if it happened to him.

Again, the teacher stops the tale, and the third person continues. Continue this process until the entire story is told. Group members may get more than one turn each.

When the group finishes the story, the class has a chance to direct questions to specific group members in an attempt to determine whose story it is.

When the questioning is completed, ask the class to vote for the person who is telling the truth.

Do this for all groups.

Discuss with students the need to make a fictional situation sound as truthful as possible. This skill, taught in an enjoyable way through this exercise, is one of the basic principles of acting.

"Mirrors"

There are three variations of this exercise.

Procedure:

Variation 1: Two people stand and face each other. One begins a *very* slow movement. The other follows as if he were a mirror image of the leader. This serves as an example to the class. Now select two other students to perform the activity. After a while, add a third student who stands diagonally across from the "follower" (or to the "leader's" side). The third student mirrors the follower. A fourth student is selected to stand opposite the third and mirror the third. This continues until the entire class is participating, all mirroring the previous student called upon—and all, although they are not looking at the original "leader," following him. The exercise should be done slowly for best results.

Variation 2: Two students sit facing each other. One is the leader and the other mirrors him. A third student asks the follower simple math questions, and a fourth asks the follower "personal" questions like, "What is your favorite TV show?" or "How many brothers do you have?" The follower must answer the questions, which may come quickly at times, and still concentrate on mirroring the leader.

Discuss the benefits of these exercises, eliciting responses concerning concentration and the need to remain relaxed even in "tense" situations.

Variation 3: This variation of the mirror exercise leads to an improvisation. Each student selects a partner. One is A and one is B. Each of the As decides upon, but does not tell his partner, a kind of job or occupation. Then the As begin to act out the job in a very slow motion.

The Bs, without asking questions or talking, try to mirror the As, thinking to themselves all the while about the actions they are performing and what job it could be. The Bs then lead the As through a different occupation. Now tell the Bs to move to one side of the room and the As to another. Each group should create an improvisation using all of the occupations that were just mirrored (which, in this case, would be the B's selected jobs).

Help the students begin planning the improvisations by asking if there is any place where these types of occupations might be found. Then work with the development of plot—the "what," "when," "who," "where."

One group—it doesn't matter which—performs its improvisation first, followed by the other. Ask questions like, "Did you recognize your partner's occupation?" "Was it what you thought it was during the mirror section of today's activities?" "Was this a creative and interesting story?" "Was the location the group chose a good one?"

Yes, talking is permitted in the improvisations!

"Chain Improvisation"

Materials: some pieces of furniture

Procedure: Tell the students that today we are going to work on improvisations which will help them learn to think quickly.

Have a student sit in front of the room. Now tell the class that someone should come up and "relate" to the person sitting before them. Try not to let the word *relate* confuse them. They may think that the relationship needs to be a familial one. Give some examples, such as teacher, hairdresser, shoe salesman, little sister, etc. When the second student comes up to the first, a plot will usually begin. If not, help them along with questions like, "Why do you want to talk to this person?" "Is there a problem that you two need to discuss or solve?"

Make sure also that the second student does not give away who he is by telling the first student outright. The first student must guess what the relationship is by what the second student chooses to say. For example, the second student may begin with, "Lisa, Mommy said you were going to take me for ice cream." Right away the first student can guess the sister-sister relationship.

After a while, ask the first student to return to his seat and tell the second student to remain in front of the class. Now a third student will come up and create a new relationship with the second. This goes on until all of the class has been involved.

This is sometimes known as a "chain improvisation" because one student always remains before the class and provides a kind of "link" from one episode to the next.

End the class with a summary of the activity. Ask the students what they thought the session taught, and also ask "how" it teaches them. Chain improvs have proven successful countless times, and I'm sure this experience will be a good one.

Extension or variation: Have one actor remain throughout the entire exercise, with each member of the class relating to him in a different way (setting and conflict/situation changing also).

Lessons 23–29

Characterization

Commentary

Many of you have begun the Scene Study Unit by now, and students are beginning to delve into the area of characterization. Even if you have chosen not to use that unit, this particular area is intrinsic to the study of acting.

Lessons 23–25 include activities which encourage actors to explore detail in creating vivid, colorful characters. I thank Sharon Halverson, who made the Hat Exercise (Lesson 23) available at the Convention of the American Alliance for Theater and Education in Portland, Oregon, in August 1988.

Lessons 26–29 are performance assignments, which must be prepared and presented by each actor. I first thought of the Painting Exercise as a valuable tool for character creation when I saw the New York production of *Sunday in the Park with George.* This musical, based upon George Seurat's painting, *A Sunday Afternoon on the Island of La Grande Jatte,* creates a magnificent still-life stage picture of the painting. Suddenly the painting comes alive before our eyes as we learn about the lives of what heretofore had been merely nameless (and some faceless) characters on canvas. I felt this would be a wonderful vehicle for creating characters of many time periods.

The Newspaper Exercise is derived from reading any major newspaper on any given day of the year, when often the most dramatic events are recounted. The teacher may want to inform the students that many playwrights, including Shakespeare, used current events in the creation of their works. (A true story concerns a student in the theater department of a university who saw the Theater secretary reading a "not so major" newspaper! He asked her what she was reading that newspaper for, and she retorted, "This is the drama department, right? Well, I'm reading the drama of the week!").

The teacher should determine whether to assign students one or both performance assignments. In a large class, where it is not feasible for every student to perform both, I have divided the class, with half doing each assignment. In this way, student actors who performed one could learn from watching the presentations of the other exercise.

Lesson 23

Creating a Character

Materials:
a number of different hats (I used nine, but fewer can be used)
a blackboard

Procedure:
This lesson focuses on creating characterization.

Part I:

The class sits before the blackboard. The hats should be visible to the class at this time.

Ask the class what type of character would wear each hat. You are looking for a noun at this point. (The hats selected for this exercise should be unique in some way. For example, a turban, a crown, an Indian headband, etc. This will encourage the students to use their imagination.) List these characters on the blackboard.

Now ask the class to describe the personality or mood of the characters listed. (Our list included a "cool, big-spending gambler," a "joyous, dance-loving babysitter from Jamaica," etc.)

The next step is to ask the class for three interesting locations, and you should write these on the board also.

Part II:

Select two students to play characters in a scene. Each should select and wear one of the hats. The class should choose one of the three listed environments.

One student will start the scene by pantomiming an activity that would take place in the chosen environment. The second character enters the scene when the environment is made clear and begins a conversation with the first character. Both actors must adopt the characters suggested by the hats they have chosen, and they must also sustain the personality or mood indicated—until something happens in the course of the scene to change it.

You may need to guide the scene to a conclusion.

You may continue this exercise with additional students added to the original improvisation, or begin a new improv. In any case, make sure that new actors select and wear a hat as they perform.

Objectives:
The student will:
- create characterization using hats
- establish place, time, and plot in an improvisational performance
- create character through voice and body movement
- listen respectfully to the ideas of others
- use the creative imagination
- contribute ideas to group planning

Lesson 24
Character Traits and Physical Emphasis

Materials:
index cards with a part of the body listed on each
index cards with a character trait written on each

Procedure:
This lesson will continue work on characterization.

Part I:
Tell students that there are many ways to create characterization. Today we will address two specific methods: emphasizing certain body parts, and emphasizing character traits.

You can give an example of the first method by citing times that people emphasize their fingers when showing off a new ring, or when women just had their nails done a very special way. Characters who are nosy, for example, may be created in a similar way: by emphasizing the ears or sometimes the nose. Demonstrate this for the class.

Have the class members choose a body-part card. (I used ears, hands, knees, neck, wrists, fingers, shoulders, hips, nose, eyes, feet.) The cards should be face down so the actor does not know what is written on them. He must then walk across the room, creating a character by emphasizing that body part. The class must guess the character and the body part.

Part II:
Discuss the definition of a character trait with the class, differentiating between it and a temporary feeling. For example, a person may be shy under certain circumstances, but that would not necessarily be a character trait. If the person is almost always shy, that is a trait.

Ask the students to choose one of the face-down traits cards. The student then comes before the class and performs an activity which demonstrates that trait. Ask another actor to choose a card and relate to the first actor, using the trait he has just chosen. Develop the plot into an improvisation. More characters and traits may be added.

At the completion of the activity, ask students to talk about character traits they recognize in themselves and in their friends, parents, teachers, etc.

Objectives:
The student will:
- understand what a character trait is
- understand what traits he has and therefore learn more about himself
- learn to incorporate traits into characterization (voice and body)
- explore the vocabulary associated with specific traits
- create character through emphasis on body parts
- learn to work in a cooperative way
- respect other contributions, opinions, etc.

Lesson 25

Improvising a Character

Materials:
list of characters (provided)
furniture for improvisation performance

Procedure:
Today's lesson continues work on characterization.

Give each student a list of characters. Each student should select a partner to work with in creating an improvisation which will be presented to the class.

The actors should choose a character that they would like to investigate. Each of the two actors working together, however, should have different characters.

Ask them where these two characters would be. What would the situation be that would bring them together? What is the conflict? How will it be solved?

The groups may work independently for ten to fifteen minutes in developing the improvisation and may then present it to the class. You may, on the other hand, want to create the improvisation as an entire class. This latter procedure would be beneficial if the class has trouble with creating improvs or has trouble working independently.

The list of characters:

- inexperienced teacher
- basketball player
- aspiring actor
- mother-in-law
- novelist
- young musician
- member of the clergy
- nosy neighbor
- teenager on first date
- strict parent

- telephone repairman
- real estate salesman
- waiter/waitress
- inexperienced magician
- gourmet chef
- rock singer
- doctor
- senior citizen
- travel agent
- political candidate

Objectives:
The student will:
- use the voice and body to create characterization
- use the creative imagination
- work cooperatively

Lesson 26
The Painting Exercise

Materials:
none

Procedure:
Begin by telling the students that an assignment will be given today. This task, although difficult, will certainly be an exciting one for both actor and audience. It is the Painting Exercise.

Discuss with the students the various methods actors use to create a character. The answers will include observation, studying the text for specific language, descriptions, inferences, etc.

Make students aware that actors learn not only by observing other human beings, but also through the study of animals and sometimes even through the study of inanimate objects. Refer to the Character Sketch Sheet (included in the Scene Study Unit, Part III of this book), which is filled out during scene study. The section entitled "Sensory and Physical Images" deals with characterization through flowers, seasons of the year, colors, types of music, etc. For this exercise we will use paintings.

Students should find a book of paintings, and they should concentrate on the realistic ones. They are to study a character in the painting in great detail. Notice the facial features, the physical silhouette of the person, etc. Ask yourself questions like, "What kind of person is this?" "How old is this person?" "What occupation is this person engaged in?" "What kind of personality does this person have?" The list is endless, but the point is to "learn" as much about this person as possible.

The student should now study the person's physical and mental attitude in the painting. What is this person doing? How does he or she feel about the activity. What is on his/her mind?

Using the exact position of the person in the painting as a starting place or an ending place, create an interesting story and act it out, with the student being the character.

Make students aware that if the painting is of another time period, as most will probably be, they must do some research. What type of suggestive costume should be used? (Too many of these assignments use characters from 1850 speaking contemporary slang.)

If dialogue is needed, create an "invisible" character to speak to.

While this exercise is an acting assignment, it also includes some historical research on costume, customs, movement and gestures, painters and their work, how to relate to invisible characters, etc.

Objectives:

The student will:
- create a character through the use of a painting
- select appropriate costuming
- select blocking, movement, and gestures of a particular time period
- create and perform a story using the character in the painting
- critique the work of his colleagues
- share ideas cooperatively and constructively

Note: The procedure for performance of this assignment will be discussed in Lesson 27. Students must bring the book of paintings to class.

Lesson 27

Performing the Painting Exercise

Materials:
brought in by students for presentation of the Painting Exercise

Procedure:
During this class (and several to follow, if class size warrants), students will present the Painting Exercise assigned in Lesson 26.

Explain the procedure to the students. The performer will show the painting (obviously, this probably will be a reproduction or photo of the painting) to the class. Students should examine the character's facial expressions and try to determine age. The clothing should give them a feel for the time period.

The actor presents the exercise.

Once again the painting is viewed by the class.

Discussion of the work follows the format used for all performance assignments: The class discusses "what they saw"; that is, the story line. The positive aspects of the exercise are noted. Perhaps the actor has truly captured the character in the painting, or maybe the time period of the painting was brought to life.

Suggestions are entertained which would make the performance stronger. The teacher works on the piece with the actor to improve one or two problems. The actor continues to work on these for all future exercises, and the teacher will move to additional areas of concern. (In this manner, the student actor is not overwhelmed with numerous problems at one time.)

Objectives:
The student will:
- present the Painting Exercise
- create a believable character
- create the time period through voice and movement
- observe the painting exercises as performed by classmates
- develop a critical eye
- develop listening skills
- critique the performance(s) through an organized procedure

Lesson 28

The Newspaper Exercise

Materials:
none

Procedure:
The Newspaper Exercise will be explained and assigned today.

The newspaper is an important tool for the actor's study of characterization. It makes him aware of many different kinds of people and their attitudes and motivations pertaining to events in daily life. Frequently, these attitudes and motivations are much different from his own, but the actor must learn to justify them through the backgrounds and perspectives of the people involved. The newspaper is also filled with items which, in themselves, might make excellent theater (and often do).

Students should research newspapers for articles to make an interesting performance. Newspapers abound with dramatic situations—hijacked airplanes, unscrupulous business deals, people reunited with loved ones after many years of being apart, palimony suits, etc.

After finding an interesting news story, the student should create a plot which can be acted out for the class. He can play any character integral to the story (not necessarily the "lead" character). Also, adjustments should be made so the plot is more interesting, or to tighten it for stage use.

Objectives:
The student will:
- create a performance based on a newspaper story
- create a believable character based on a newspaper story
- select appropriate material from the article in constructing a plot
- use his creative imagination
- use costumes, props, and setting to create a believable story

Lesson 29
Performing the Newspaper Exercise

Materials:
brought in by students for presentation of the Newspaper Exercise

Procedure:
During this and succeeding classes students will present the Newspaper Exercise assigned in Lesson 28.

Explain the procedure to the class. The performer will present the exercise (which is a short scene based on a newspaper article). The actor may be any character involved with the story, and not necessarily the main character. The article may be used as a "springboard" for a closely related incident and therefore does not have to follow the article precisely.

After the performance, the actor reads the article to the class.

Discussion of the work follows the format used for all post-perform- ance dialogue: The class discusses "what they saw"; that is, the story line. They may want to discuss the actor's interpretation, especially if it differs from the straight facts of the article.

The positive aspects of the exercise are noted. Suggestions are entertained which would make the performance stronger, and the teacher works on the piece with the actor to improve one or two problems. The actor continues to work on these for all future exercises, and the teacher will move to additional areas of concern. (In this manner the student actor is not overwhelmed with numerous problems at one time.)

Objectives:
The student will:
- present the Newspaper Exercise
- interpret a newspaper article
- create a story line and bring it to life through voice and movement
- observe the newspaper exercises as performed by classmates
- develop listening skills
- develop a critical eye
- critique the performance(s)

Part II
Advanced Acting

The Great White Hope by Howard Sackler

Advanced Acting

Advanced Acting expands upon the actor's growth begun in the Introductory Course. It is obviously more specialized in that it offers students a more in-depth, cumulative, progressive study of acting. This course differs from the introductory level in four ways:

More individual performance assignments are provided for students.

Two scenes are studied and performed, rather than one. The first is a psychophysical, or dramatic, scene, and the second is a comedy. These scenes are more demanding than those of the previous course. The students should also be more aware of various acting elements and infuse these into their scene study performances. These include a rich subtext, sense memory, emotional recall, a sense of pre- and post-scene, and assimilation.

Voice and speech work is introduced.

There are a good number of relaxation and self-discovery exercises—relaxation because it is only in that state that creativity and imagination are at their peak, and self-discovery because I feel an actor should know himself before trying to become someone else.

Advanced Acting reinforces the basic concepts of trust and sharing, and offers wonderful opportunities for creative thought as well as exciting performances. While it is an accelerated course, it should also provide fun and excitement. Student progress should be evident throughout, and performances should be of a high caliber. The lessons are more detailed, as they focus on specific facets of acting training. Additional individual performances afford the acting teacher the opportunity to get to know his students to an even greater extent than before, and to experience the joy of witnessing their own self-discovery through these lessons while creating a clearer perception of themselves in their community and their world.

Lesson 1

The Social Repertoire Exercise

Commentary

Just as the Apology Lesson began the Introductory Course with action and student involvement, the Social Repertoire Exercise is a fun-filled activity with which to begin the Advanced Course. First, a discussion of what "fine acting" is should be guided by the teacher to a realization that an actor's development parallels his growth in self-awareness, and that he has to know about himself in order to use this knowledge to create a character.

An exercise that demonstrates this fact is the Social Repertoire as it appears in Robert L. Benedetti's excellent book, *The Actor at Work.* During this activity the players learn a great deal about themselves in relation to six major personality elements. The teacher should provide enough time after the exercise for both participants and observers to comment on the degree of comfort or discomfort felt toward each of the elements. The class may come upon some startling discoveries: that a particularly shy student is very attracted to the role of the "bully," or that a student will suddenly understand that he's been unconsciously playing the role of the "Red Cross nurse" too long and it has created a great deal of stress! Make sure that the observers participate as well by asking them such questions as "What role do you think would have been most comfortable for you?" or "What role might you have avoided?" The observers should learn as much as the participants in this exercise.

I have included a Social Repertoire Chart that I devised to complement and extend this lesson. The chart should be filled in by the students for two days, preferably a school day and a non-school day. When giving directions pertaining to its completion, give some examples of the various roles we play each day and the accompanying physical adjustments—how the student who hasn't done the homework may shrink in his seat, how the football hero may loom larger than life as he struts down the hallway—and vocal adjustments—how our vocabulary and general voice quality differ when talking to a close friend as opposed to an angry employer or teacher. The last column asks whether the student actor is comfortable or uncomfortable in that role.

This lesson should make student actors aware of the many roles all human beings play in their everyday relationships. These can and should be tapped for use on the stage.

Materials:
index cards for the Social Repertoire Game (prepared prior to class)
Social Repertoire Charts (following this lesson)

Procedure:

Part I:
Welcome students to the class. Tell them that Advanced Acting will continue the training that they began in the Introductory Course. Explain the course objectives and give a brief outline of the course of study: a psychophysical (dramatic) acting unit, including scene; a comedy unit, including scene for study and performance; and a unit on theater voice and diction.

Part II:
Ask the students what they feel are characteristics of good acting. You will probably elicit such responses as "acting which is believable," "acting in which the performers are committed to their work," etc.

After the students have shared their responses, explain that actors have to get to know themselves before they can truly "become" another character.

Introduce the Social Repertoire Game. Six volunteers sit in a circle and are told that they are to discuss a project they will undertake together. It can be something like going on a picnic, planning a dance, putting on a show, etc.

Give each one of the six students one of the following roles to play in the activity planning. (The roles are explained on large index cards and actually given to each student):

CHAIRPERSON: tends to organize

BULLY: doesn't care what the group does as long as it does what he wants!

VICTIM: sees any group action as unpleasant or threatening

RED CROSS NURSE: takes care of anyone who needs help, whether he wants it or not

DE-RAILER: forever changes the topic as a way of controlling the group

PHILOSOPHER: loves to point out the deeper meaning

Students begin planning, playing the roles described on the card before them. Let the discussion continue for a few minutes. Then ask each student to pass his card to the person on his right.

Each student must now assume the new role on the received index card. Allow the game to continue until each student has played all six roles.

Ask questions such as: "What role did you feel most comfortable with?" "Least comfortable with?" "Were you surprised at any of the feelings that you were previously unaware of?" "Did anyone anger you while playing a specific role?" "What did you learn about yourself while playing this game?"

This is a wonderful game to help students discover how many different roles they play. Explain that there are numerous other roles also. Give each student the Social Repertoire Chart. Ask them to fill out the charts for two days and then bring them to class for discussion. The chart will make them aware of the physical and vocal adjustments that accompany the various roles we play every day.

Objectives:
The student will:
- learn about goals of the course
- become aware of the course outline and units of study
- learn some of the major elements of acting training
- learn that we play many roles each day
- learn that we can use the roles we play for creating other characters

Social Repertoire Chart

Role	Day	Time	Physical Adjustment (include sense of size, weight, attractiveness)	Vocal Adjustment (include language choice, volume, tone, etc.)	Comf/Uncomf

Lessons 2–4
Actions

Commentary

Part I of Lesson 2 provides a quick and clever way to learn the names of your class members. Since, however, this is the second course in a sequence, it is quite possible that most or all of your students are familiar with each other. In this case, you may introduce one of the many closely related varieties of this memorization game: create a fictional name; create a fictional name and add a birthplace; or create a fictional name, a birthplace, and an occupation.

Using the same format as the example given in the lesson, the first person says, "We're going on a picnic and I'm bringing a ———." The second person says, "We're going on a picnic and I'm bringing a ——— and he's [referring to the first person] bringing a ———." As the exercise continues, each class member adds an item and the list grows longer. These theater games provide a unique structure for teaching the concentration and memorization skills needed in acting.

The action work found in Part II is a review, reinforcement, and continuation of those skills in relation to attaining stage truth and believability. Often exercises in this section of the book will bear this relationship to work found in the Introductory Course because acting skills are cumulative, sequential, and interrelated.

Lessons 3 and 4 continue the study of actions. Here, however, the actions are rehearsed rather than improvisational, as they are based on circumstances from established plays. A special feature of this assignment is that it makes these plays accessible to many inexperienced actors and may motivate them to read more plays. The rehearsed sequence of actions may be compared to the notes on a musician's sheet of music, where the artist plays precise notes which, when played sequentially, produce a desired effect. This lesson is, then, a more formal study of the relationships among the natural progression of actions in telling a story. Additional examples and explanation can be found in Charles McGaw's *Acting Is Believing*, another truly fine book on acting technique. McGaw refers to this sequence of actions as a "score."

The importance of actions cannot be underestimated. Of the three techniques used to develop character—what a character says, what others say about him, and what a character does—the last is the most truthful and effective method on the stage. Certainly a person's actions warrant remembering. On stage and in life, character is always revealed through one's choices.

An actor's task is to create the physical life of the character. He determines what type of person the character is and then creates the physical life through sequential and believable actions. It is from these actions, performed through proper motivation and in the given circumstances of the play, that emotion is evoked and the audience is affected.

An interesting observation about actions and their ability to create emotion was recently made by an advanced acting student of mine while writing a self-evaluation form. He felt that he had been melodramatic in a scene and, after much consideration, attributed this to ". . . a tendency to play an emotion itself rather than my character's action under the influence of the emotion. I am broadcasting my own reaction to the script and the situation rather than . . . creating the situation so realistically that the emotion is elicited in my audience. For instance, in a script's most poignant moments the characters may be completely unaware of the emotionality of their situation. They are not looking at themselves; they are not self-conscious. However, the audience/reactor will interpret the poignancy of the scene and be affected by it."

We may ask where the actions come from. The text obviously supplies many—both stated directly and implied—and many come from the actor's creative imagination. All actions, however, must make sense; that is, they must be performed in proper order, producing a believable and truthful situation.

Lesson 2

Truth and Believability

Materials:
Action Worksheet (following this lesson)

Procedure:

Part I:
Tell the students that we will begin class today by playing a game which will help us learn each other's name.

Have the entire class sit in a circle. If space permits, it is better to sit on the floor or a carpet to break down the "formality" of the class.

The leader begins by introducing himself to the class. "Hello, my name is _____ ." The person to the leader's right says, "Hello, my name is _____ and this is _____ ." The second person referred to by the student is the leader. The third student introduces himself, the second student, and the leader. The game continues until everyone has introduced himself and everyone in proper order after him. Obviously the game gets more difficult as it progresses. It is an interesting way to get the class to become acquainted, and it also requires involvement!

Part II:
Pass out the Action Worksheets. Read the directions to the class. In essence, they state that actions must be truthful and believable. Also, actions evoke feeling.

Tell the class to select one of the actions, and plan to perform that action in front of the class. Give them a few minutes to plan it out.

As each student performs, be positive in your comments. Find good things to say about the performance. Be constructive in the criticisms and offer suggestions for improvement. Have the student try the actions in different ways, illustrating and noting the improvements, all of which are aimed at achieving truthfulness.

Objectives:
The student will:
- learn the names of other students in the class
- learn that actions must be truthful and believable
- learn that actions evoke feelings

Action Worksheet

An action by itself is a means to reach an objective. Coupled with the character's desire to reach that objective, however, actions can have startling results and make us feel powerful emotions. Rehearse the actions that you feel will illustrate the following activities, giving them detail and orderly and believable sequence, and making sure they are dictated by a sense of inner truth.

- watering the plants in your apartment, when one begins to overflow onto the floor

- studying for an exam and trying to ignore the ringing telephone

- paddling a canoe through both calm and rough stretches of a river

- feeding birds in a park

- petting and caring for a sick animal

- trying to select for purchase one CD, tape or record album among many

- digging a hole and burying an important object

- sewing a hem on an article of clothing you want to wear tonight, knowing you will be picked up momentarily by friends

- taking your first driving lesson with an irritable instructor

- eating hot pizza

Lesson 3
Sequential Actions

Materials:
Sequential Actions Worksheet
Sequential Actions Worksheet for *Cyrano de Bergerac*

Procedure:

Part I:
Review with students the details of actions and how they must be specific rather than general. Today we will deal with a logical sequence of actions that produce a believable situation.

You may want to compare this sequence to a musician's score where the artist plays precise notes every time which, when played sequentially, create a desired effect.

Where does this sequence of actions come from? Some actions are written into the play by the playwright; some are implied in the text; some are created by the actor as he brings his character to life.

Go over the list of sequential actions that comprise *Cyrano de Bergerac* on the worksheet. Note the listed actions, with one leading logically to the next.

Ask if there are any questions. If not, proceed to the list of circumstances on the following pages. You may read these aloud.

For homework, select one of the listed circumstances and create sequential actions for it to be performed for the class. These actions must be written out in list form, rehearsed thoroughly, and performed.

Part II:
Tell the students that they will now deal with the following scene.

You are a government agent who must steal top-secret plans from a terrorist whose objective is to blow up a major U.S. landmark. The terrorist is sleeping in a well-guarded room. You have managed to get in, but there are windows with guards just outside. The document is in the breast pocket of the sleeping man.

As a group effort, with the leader as guide, create the environment. Specific areas must be designated for the bed, the windows, the door, etc. What should happen first? What second, and so forth?

What details should we be aware of? What about noise, etc.? Create questions which attend to details that the class should be aware of. Have a volunteer, or perhaps more than one, perform this sequence of actions.

Objectives:
The student will:
- learn the principles of sequence and logic
- work cooperatively and share ideas
- continue work on details in acting

Sequential Actions Worksheet

for *Cyrano de Bergerac* by Edmond Rostand

Let us examine a sequence of actions based upon a moment in *Cyrano de Bergerac*. The play takes place in France in 1640, and in it we meet one of the most colorful characters in dramatic literature. Cyrano is desperately in love with the beautiful Roxanne, but he feels he cannot express his love to her face, as his large nose is an impediment to his love life. In Act II, scene iii, Cyrano is in the bake shop of his friend Ragueneau, where he awaits his 7 o'clock meeting with Roxanne. He has decided to write a letter to profess his love.

A possible sequence of actions for this moment might be:

1. Cyrano enters the bake shop hurriedly.
2. He immediately looks to the clock to learn the time.
3. He paces, wondering how he can adequately tell Roxanne of his love for her.
4. He decides to write a letter.
5. Cyrano nervously sits down at a table.
6. He asks Ragueneau for a pen and a sheet of paper ("invisible" characters may be used and addressed).
7. Cyrano hears someone enter the shop and quickly looks to the door, but it is not Roxanne.
8. He picks up the pen and waves Ragueneau away so that he may write in privacy.
9. He begins to write.
10. After a short while, he throws his pen down as he loses the courage to express his feelings.
11. He asks Ragueneau what time it is.
12. He decides he must write, and picks up the pen again.
13. He is heard murmuring, "I love you."
14. He continues to write, murmuring at times "Your eyes" and "Your lips."
15. He closes the letter with "Your faithful worshipper."
16. Cyrano stops as he is about to sign his name, stands up, and puts the letter in his doublet.
17. He goes to the door to see if Roxanne is arriving.
18. He waves Ragueneau and his company into another room as Roxanne approaches the door.
19. Cyrano throws open the door, bowing deeply as he says, "Come in!"

Sequential Actions Worksheet

From *Picnic,* by William Inge

Madge, the beautiful daughter of Flo Owens, gives herself a manicure and flips through a magazine to pass the time on Labor Day afternoon in Kansas in the early 1950s.

From *Much Ado About Nothing,* by William Shakespeare

Benedick, a "professional bachelor," hides in the palace gardens, eavesdropping on two friends. Knowing he is hiding, they try to trick him into falling in love with Beatrice, his adversary, by claiming that they know that Beatrice loves Benedick but is afraid to admit it. Benedick is startled at the news.

From *The Prime of Miss Jean Brodie,* by Jay Presson Allen (adapted from the novel by Muriel Spark)

Sandy, one of Jean Brodie's students, tries to impress her teacher by helping to prepare a picnic prior to Jean's arrival. She works quickly to spread the blanket, set up a stool for Miss Brodie to sit upon, and examine the contents of the picnic basket.

From *Desire Under the Elms,* by Eugene O'Neill

Eben Cabot sneaks into the bedroom shared by his father and Abbie, old Cabot's new and much younger wife. Eben goes to the cradle which holds the illegitimate child Eben and Abbie have had and gently rocks it, gazing down proudly and lovingly at his newborn son.

From *Look Homeward, Angel,* by Ketti Frings (adapted from the novel by Thomas Wolfe)

On a beautiful summer evening in 1916, Eugene Gant strolls out of his mother's boardinghouse and sits on the porch. He hears a distant train whistle "moan mournfully" and thinks about the excitement of traveling to faraway places.

From *All My Sons,* by Arthur Miller

Chris Keller is busy chopping up a tree downed by violent winds the night before. He breaks the tree into manageable pieces and drags them to the side of the house.

From *The Little Foxes,* by Lillian Hellman

Regina Giddens is returning to her large Southern home in the spring of 1900. She has previously had a huge argument with her husband, Horace. She enters the home with her wet umbrella and cloak, both of which she must dispose of. She then notices her husband's safe deposit box and goes to it to examine its contents, only to be stopped by the voice of Horace.

From *Steel Magnolias,* by Robert Harling

Truvy Jones, the owner of a small beauty parlor in Louisiana, sweeps around the hair-styling station and prepares for her next client by cleaning combs and setting out towels, hair clips, brushes, and scissors.

From *The Shadow Box,* by Michael Cristofer

Taking place in one of several cottages devoted to terminally ill patients, this excerpt shows Mark sitting on a couch. He checks his watch, rises and goes to the bookcase. He begins to prepare some medicine located there, but instead he picks up the tray with the medicine and throws it violently.

From *The Heidi Chronicles,* by Wendy Wasserstein

Heidi is at a high school dance in 1965. She finds a corner where she looks out at the dance floor and sways to the music. When her girlfriend leaves to dance, Heidi sits on a chair, takes out a book, and puts it on her lap as she stares out at the other students enjoying themselves. Soon a young man sits next to her. She smiles and looks down.

Lesson 4

Performing Sequential Actions

Materials:
brought in by students for performance of the sequential action assignment

Procedure:
Today students will present the sequential action performance from Lesson 3. These performances will obviously take more than one period. Make the performance schedule according to your specific instructional design. That is, if your class is relatively small, two or three successive periods of presentation may be fine. With larger groups, I often intersperse these periods with other lessons. This adds variety to the overall course.

Explain the format you will use for the performance of the score.

After the presentation, the class will critique the scene.

There is a definite and specific method for any performance critique. Note the pages on "Post-Performance Critique" in the Scene Study, Part III of this book. This format is used for all acting courses.

The student should read aloud the list of actions he was required to write as part of the assignment. Note should be made of the detail used.

Use this method for all performances.

Objectives:
The student will:
- perform the score using detail in body movement/gestures and voice (if necessary)
- practice the method of critiquing a performance
- share ideas for improvement of performances

Lesson 5

Actions and Sense Memory

Commentary

The Introductory Course devoted Lessons 5–8 to sensory awareness. Lesson 5 of the Advanced Course reinforces this idea in order to make our stage work more truthful. Previously, the senses were used in connection with simple activities, such as sniffing various bottles of perfume or tasting a particular food in an imaginary delicatessen. Now the "plot" of the exercise is developed a bit more, requiring a more complex sequence of actions and a more intensive use of the senses.

It might also be interesting to begin class by asking the students to discuss any strong sensory experience they have had recently, such as the strong smell of chemicals in a science lab, a beautiful sunset or sunrise, or a particularly delicious meal in a restaurant. It is a good idea to make actors aware that they should store these moments away in that cache of "inner resources" which is drawn upon over and over again for stage use.

Materials:

Procedure:

Today we will continue our work with determining a logical sequence of actions, and add sense memory to it.

Review with students the concept of sense memory, introduced in Lesson 5 of the Introductory Course. Ask them what part the senses play in their acting now. Elicit responses about the importance of the senses in our work.

Tell them that today we will combine our work with a logical sequence of actions and the senses. Students will perform the following exercises.

Exercise 1: A person helps a sick dog deliver pups.

Exercise 2: A person discovers a tunnel which has not been used for hundreds of years under an old monastery.

Exercise 3: A person is on a whale-watching boat on a brisk morning in early summer. The sea is very calm and there seems to be no activity. Suddenly, from seemingly nowhere, a huge whale surfaces extremely close to the boat and startles the person.

Exercise 4: A person enters the crypt where members of an aristocratic family have been buried for centuries.

Exercise 5: A person feeds the giant wild birds in their cage at the zoo.

Exercise 6: A person accidentally discovers a cache of jewels on a Caribbean island.

Objectives:

The student will:
- create a logical sequence of actions using detail in body movement/gestures and voice (if necessary)
- integrate the use of the senses in the sequence of actions
- understand the importance of the senses in acting
- share ideas for improvement of performances

Lessons 6–7
The Dialogue Exercise

Commentary

These lessons return to the Dialogue Exercise, the source of much creativity and enjoyment in the Introductory Course. Review the rules of this exercise listed in the lesson plan, emphasizing the need to motivate every line and action. Students will find out that this dialogue is longer and, indeed, more complex than the previous ones. Encourage the use of costumes and props, as these add humor, color, and excitement to the activity.

In addition, determine whether your class needs to "brainstorm" an example together. Often, a less experienced group benefits from this, as it clarifies the procedure and requirements. A more advanced group, on the other hand, is usually eager to get right to work, feeling that brainstorming "steals" their ideas.

Lesson 6
Creating a Sequence of Actions

Materials:
Dialogue Worksheets (following this lesson)

Procedure:

Part I:
Review with students the concept that any logical sequence of actions has a specific reason for performing them.

Everything we do and say onstage must be justified.

Pass out the accompanying Dialogue Worksheet. Tell the class that this is a dialogue for two people, A and B.

These lines are the basis for a sequence of actions which the students, in pairs, must create on their own. Some of the "rules" to be aware of are:

- there must be a reason to say every line

- there must be a reason for every action the students create to the accompanying lines

- the order of the lines may not be changed

- no words may be added or deleted

- sounds (laughs, cries, moans, etc.) are permissible

- costumes and props are highly encouraged

Ask the class if there are any questions.

Part II:
Give some class time for students to select a partner and work on their "scenes." The amount of class time is determined by the leader. You may need to give about 20 minutes on two consecutive days, or one entire class period, etc. *Encourage originality and fun!*

Objectives:
The student will:
- learn to justify dialogue and actions
- use his creative imagination
- share his ideas with a partner
- cooperate

Dialogue Worksheet

A: *Wasn't that the greatest?*

B: *I don't know. I've had more fun.*

A: *Give me a break! Doing what, for instance?*

B: *Well, did you ever try this?*

A: *That looks difficult.*

B: *Try it.*

A: *Let's see . . . oh, I can't.*

B: *Try it again. And use this. It may help.*

A: *OK. How am I doing?*

B: *Oh, wow!*

A: *Hey, I think there's a problem!*

B: *Be careful. Be careful!*

A: *Help!*

B: *Hold on.*

A: *So, how did I do?*

B: *Let's go to a movie.*

Lesson 7

Performing the Dialogue Exercise

Materials:
brought in by students for the presentation of the dialogue assignment (Lesson 6)

Procedure:
Review with students the objectives of the dialogue assignment: *that every line and action in a scene must be justified.*

On the first presentation day of this assignment, I usually give the class approximately ten minutes to review their work with their partners. Also, the time may be necessary for any costume changes, prop preparation, etc.

Call the class back for the performances. You may want to assign an order of that day's performances.

After each performance discuss the project using the following criteria: Were all lines and actions justified? What section was most difficult to justify? Was the creative imagination used? What did the class most enjoy about the performance? Were the actors visible at all times?

Obviously, the sophistication of the critique will be determined by the experience of the class.

All critiques should follow the format discussed in the section on sequential actions in Lesson 4.

Objectives:
The student will:
- learn to justify all lines and actions
- exercise his imagination and creativity
- learn the format of a performance critique
- use the body and voice to create a character

Lessons 8–11

Relaxation, the Key to Creativity

Commentary

Relaxation is important in acting—as it is in life in general. We need only look around us to witness the numerous tension-causing elements of our lives—relationships, lack of time, commitments, bills, homework, peer pressure, money. Obviously, the actor is not immune to these aspects of contemporary civilization. The pace of life is fast and often fraught with conflict. There seems to be no time or opportunity to slow down.

But our art demands just that. How can we achieve a creative state? How can the actor rid his body and mind of destructive tensions in order to do his work? How can we explore and discover new (or existing) aspects of ourselves with which to build a character when we are racked by the often overwhelming pressures of daily living?

Relaxation is a way of regaining a connection to one's body and mind. Through the exercises that follow, the actor learns a different side of his craft. Here stage areas and body positions play no part; vocal quality also is unimportant. In short, the "mechanics" of acting to which we have devoted so much time are not involved. Now we exercise the mind so that it learns to concentrate, so that it can create and control the sensations we feel as actors. I say "as actors" because, as the theater is a reflection of life, it is our job to feel these sensations— sensorily and emotionally—and communicate them at a moment's notice to a body of spectators. Relaxation rids the body and mind of tension and replaces it with energy so that this communication is possible. Relaxation enables a more holistic approach to our work so that every nuance of the character's life is fresh and real and true.

These next classes are devoted to exercises which reduce tension. I suppose the most expedient way of illustrating how soothing and beneficial these exercises are is to do them immediately, with a brief discussion of the theory beforehand. Afterward, however, allow suffi- cient time for students to discuss their respective states of relaxation, the sensations they experienced, etc.

There are a few points to keep in mind:

First of all, prepare a good relaxation tape. Choose your music carefully. You will need tapes lasting approximately 10 to 15 minutes each. Please note that this tape is optional, as many people prefer to do these exercises in a quiet setting.

There will be a good amount of lying down during these exercises, so a carpeted area is desirable, or perhaps you can get mats (remnants) from a local carpet store.

Occasionally a student will actually fall asleep during these exercises! Wake him up gently, without startling him or disrupting the class. Impress upon the class that these exercises make them more alert, responsive, and full of positive energy; they should not put the students to sleep! (Once, a student of mine, a mother of three teenage boys, told me that relaxation exercises were her favorite part of acting class because they afforded her an opportunity to get the sleep she often missed due to worrying about her children! I told her that no matter how enjoyable the exercises were, sleep was not the goal, at least in acting class. Relaxation, however, has many valid uses in a wide variety of situations. Like much theatrical training, these exercises have general applications for everyone.)

Plan your time carefully so that class does not end while you are in the middle of an exercise. It is important to have "closure," affording students a smooth transition from the exercise back to the "real world," so to speak, and also to give them the opportunity to talk about the effects of the exercise.

Last, you should be relaxed when you lead these exercises. Your students will "play off" you, your tone of voice, your physicality, and your body language. If you are tense, disturbed, or overly worried about something, you will not be able to help your students achieve a state of true relaxation.

I always enjoy these relaxation exercises. The combination of their objective, a stress-free environment, and soothing music produce a wonderful class.

The Balloon Trip Exercise used in Lesson 9 is adapted from Louis John Dezseran's book *The Student Actor's Handbook* and is a very effective exercise that actors find particularly beneficial.

Lesson 8
Getting Rid of Tension

Materials:
tape recorder
tape of relaxing music lasting approximately 10 to 15 minutes

Procedure:
Ask the class to stand and spread throughout the space. Lead them through some basic warm-ups (i.e., spine folds, shake-outs, head rolls, etc. Refer to Relaxation/Exercises Warm-Up in the Scene Study Unit).

After approximately 5 or 10 minutes, introduce the concept of relaxation to the class. You may start with the very reason the class just did a short workout: to get rid of tensions that can impede the learning process.

The enormous work of the actor—the task of communicating emotions, attitudes, relationships, etc.—can only be accomplished when the body and the mind work harmoniously and are free from tensions which interfere with the dramatic tensions the actor wants to create.

We must, therefore, be able to relax both the body and the mind so that they will work for us. Also, in this relaxed state, the mind is most creative.

We will, therefore, do several "relaxation" exercises over the next few days. Our first one will be the Sun Exercise.

Everyone should lie down and align the body (the small of the back should be in a straight line with the back of the neck). The student should be as comfortable as possible.

As you lead the students through this exercise, take your time. Your voice should be soothing. It is important for *you* to be relaxed for this exercise to work. Be supportive and encouraging.

The Sun Exercise
Tell the student that he is on the beach in the summer. It is not an extremely hot or humid day but rather a warm, comfortable one. The beach is fairly empty, so no one will interfere with the actor's privacy. The sun is overhead, and during the passage of time its warm and comforting rays will come in contact with different parts of the body, relaxing them and eliminating all tensions. The actor will have to concentrate on all areas of the body mentioned by the teacher as he inhales deeply, tightening the muscles there, and

allows the tensions in that area to ride out of the body on the exhale, relaxing the muscles.

The parts of the body you will have students direct their breathing to are (from head to toe, in sequence):

the top of the head	the arms (right
the forehead	down to the fingers)
the eyes	the stomach
the jaw (it falls	the groin
open on the exhale)	the knees
the neck	the lower legs
the shoulders	the toes
the chest	

Follow this with five relaxed but deep breaths. Then play the music you have selected as "relaxation" music for about 10 minutes. Speak to the students as they are in this relaxed state. Direct their attention to the fact that they are not sleepy but rather alert and refreshed. They are more sensitive to sound and the temperature of the air, more comfortable than they have been for a long time.

Talk to the class about this exercise. Let them tell you how they feel. Are they relaxed? Did they enjoy this? Relate this state to the state an actor should be in for rehearsals and performances.

Objectives:

The student will:
- learn that the body and mind must be unified so they can work together
- learn that the body and mind communicate feelings, emotions, attitudes, relationships, etc.
- learn the importance of relaxation
- relax physically and mentally

Lesson 9

The Balloon Trip

Materials:

"relaxation" tape of soothing
music (about 15 minutes)

a broom
a scrub brush

Procedure:

Part I:

Review with students the need for mental and physical relaxation on stage. Tell them that we will do another relaxation exercise today.

Begin by having the students spread themselves throughout the space. Lead some basic warm-up exercises (use some that were not used for the previous lesson's warm-ups: head roll, swaying from the hips, basic stretches, etc. It would be a good idea to use the spine fold again, since this is one of the most beneficial of all exercises).

Have students lie down in the space, allowing a comfortable amount of room between them. They should align the body (see Lesson 8).

This exercise is called the "Balloon Trip." Each student should see a large balloon hovering at the ceiling directly above. The student may imagine the balloon to be a specific color—something soothing and relaxing. The balloon begins to drift down toward the student very slowly. The student should imagine its size, shape, texture, weight, and color as it moves steadily downward.

Finally the balloon makes contact with the student's chest. It is very light. By altering the body only slightly, the student may move the balloon down toward the knees and then back to the chest. Say to the class, "Wouldn't it be wonderful to be part of this balloon and glide ever so lightly through the air?"

Tell the students to use their imagination as they begin to "slide" into the skin of their respective balloons. The feeling is a "tingling" one, but a liberating one. There is no fear.

Once the students have become the balloon's "skin," the balloon begins to rise in the air, drifting slowly toward the ceiling. Students should be aware of changes in temperature, and the invisible air currents which gently move them along.

Direct the "balloons" to drift "through" the ceiling and into the open air above. They are now outside. Tell them to smell the air and notice yet another change in temperature as they glide upward.

Tell them that they may now travel wherever they like, and that after a while you will call them back. They should look over the surrounding neighborhoods, look down upon birds, etc.

At this point begin the relaxation music if you wish. It should have a "fresh" and "liberating" feel to it. Select the music wisely.

After a few minutes (or longer if you choose), guide the students (or rather, balloons) back over the building and lead them down to the exact space where their human bodies were before the "trip." Slowly lead them out of the balloon's skin, feet first and head last. A very deep breath is a good way to end this exercise.

It is difficult to predict how much time is needed for the exercise. I find that it usually takes about 25 minutes, but you may certainly alter it for your specific purposes.

After the students sit up slowly and without allowing tension to reenter the body, have them share their feelings about this exercise. Were they truly relaxed? Could they feel the changes in temperature, air currents, etc.? Did they feel liberated and comfortable? How does this relaxed state compare to falling asleep? to dreaming? Ask if anyone has studied Zen or yoga or meditation and ask for a comparison among the relaxed states.

Part II:

If time permits, this next activity is a fun way to end class—especially after the relaxation exercise. Ask the students to sit on the floor, and put a broom in the center of the space. Ask a volunteer to come forward and use the broom as if it were another object (a guitar, skis, javelin, etc.). The class should guess what the object is. A variation to try is to time a student for thirty seconds and have him use the broom to represent as many objects as possible in that time. You can also do this activity with a scrub brush, a vacuum cleaner hose, or almost anything else.

Objectives:

The student will:
- relax mentally and physically
- learn the need for relaxation in acting
- think spontaneously
- improve concentration abilities
- think creatively
- work cooperatively and share ideas

Lesson 10
The Tension Drain

Materials:
a tape of relaxation music lasting approximately 10 to 15 minutes (optional)

Procedure:

Part I:
Tell the class that today we will do the third of our relaxation exercises. It is called the "Tension Drain."

Begin class with a basic warm-up as you have done for Lessons 8 and 9. It may be a good idea to select new warm-ups or vary the ones you have been using. This will add variety to this all-important section of the lesson.

Part II:
Students should sit in chairs with their feet firmly on the ground and their hands resting comfortably on their thighs. If you are using seats in an auditorium, ask the students to leave an empty seat between them. This provides the sense of space so important in relaxation exercises.

Tell the students that we will rid the body of harmful stress and tensions, and that they should listen to your voice as you once again trace the flow of tension in an orderly way, progressing from the top of the head to the toes of feet. They should think of the tension in some "tangible" way. For example, make it a blue fluid, or a feeling of heat, or mercury as in a thermometer.

Begin at the head and methodically "talk the tension out of the body." Begin by saying something to the effect of, "The tension is in the top of your head. Feel it moving slowly down . . . over the forehead . . . slowly. Feel the tension draining downwards . . . over your eyebrows. Concentrate on your right eyebrow. Now the left eyebrow. Feel the tension drain from the body . . ." etc. Speak clearly and in an easy, relaxed manner, repeating the phrase "The tension is draining" periodically throughout the exercise. Make sure that all body parts are mentioned, including the nose, lips, jaw, neck, shoulders, biceps, elbows, forearms, chest, stomach, waist, hips, thighs, groin, upper legs, knees, calves, ankles, soles of the feet, and toes.

Spend only as much time on each body part as necessary, giving enough opportunity for the students to concentrate on this area. Rushing through this exercise will increase tension, so take your time.

When all tension has left the body, start your taped music. Instruct students to "relax . . . relax . . . relax." Remind them that they are not sleepy. Rather, they are more awake and alert than ever, conscious of all stimuli, including sounds, temperature, the sound of your voice, etc.

After a few minutes, tell students to concentrate on the flow of bright, life-giving energy that will "come through the floor and travel upward through the body." Tell them "We are not bringing back tension. We are allowing energy into the body."

When you focus on the body parts in this section, bring the energy into the area faster than you led the tension out. Say things like, "Feel the energy moving through the floor into your toes. Now it is in the souls of your feet and is moving upward to your ankles. Now it is moving up your calves to your knees," etc.

When energy has filled the body, have students take two deep breaths with full-bodied exhales. The students should feel and look noticeably more relaxed.

Part III:

Ask students to share their feelings about this exercise. Did they like it? Did it relax them? Could they feel the tension drain from the body? Did they feel that they had control of their tensions?

Part IV:

If time permits, you may want to end class with a theater game as a cooling-down activity (refer to "Theater Games," Introductory Course, Lesson 22).

Objectives:

The student will:
- control the tension flow in the body
- relax physically and mentally

Lesson 11

The Back Massage

Materials:

a tape of relaxation music lasting approximately 25 minutes (optional)

Procedure:

Part I:

The fourth relaxation exercise is a back-massage. Explain that actors carry a great deal of tension in the back and shoulders. A properly administered massage can greatly relieve this problem.

The instructor should demonstrate the back massage technique prior to students performing it. Ask for a student volunteer and have him stand with his back toward you. The class should stand in positions where they can easily watch your demonstration. Explain the technique as you demonstrate.

The person performing the massage should shake out the hands well prior to beginning the massage to loosen up the fingers and rid them of tension.

Place four fingers of each hand on your partner's shoulders, leaving the thumbs free to begin the massage. Alternate several circular motions with your right and left thumbs, applying pressure to relax the muscles of the upper back between the shoulders. Apply enough pressure, but not so much that you will cause discomfort to your partner.

Widen the circular motions with the thumbs until you can go no wider. At this point, continue the massage with the palms of your hands, still alternating a few circular motions at a time with each palm.

Widen the area covered to include the shoulders and upper arms. When you feel you have relaxed a large portion of the upper back, use a thumb to "rub out" muscular knots, caused by tension, along the sides of the spine.

Repeat the entire procedure.

In addition to standing, this massage may be performed in sitting positions as well. Some of my students enjoy lying face down with the masseuse straddling the waist. The main idea is comfort and safety for both the masseuse and the partner.

Part II:

Students should pair off and begin the massage. Play the prepared tape of relaxation music.

I often ask both partners in the advanced class to hum softly as the massage is performed. I also tell them to focus their breathing on the point of physical contact in the massage. This forms a bond between the two partners, as they give and receive energy from each other.

After a given amount of time (approximately 15 minutes), the partners should change positions so that the person receiving the massage will now administer it.

When this activity is complete, it is a good idea to ask the partners to thank each other. As this is a physical activity, I ask them to give a "nonverbal" sign of gratitude—a hand squeeze, a hug, etc. This continues the bonding process and increases trust between the partners.

Objectives:

The student will
- learn the procedure of massage for relaxation
- relax physically and mentally

Lesson 12

Staying in the Present

Commentary

The finest acting should not look like "acting" as the layman thinks of it. It should appear simple, unforced, and the actor should look as if he were merely "living on the stage." His work should never look rehearsed but should give the impression that it is happening for the first time! It should appear charged with spontaneity and freshness. And should we venture back to the theater to see the same play twice, the acting should still look inspired and spontaneous.

The stream-of-consciousness exercises in this lesson train actors to stay in what our contemporary culture has termed "the here and now." Eric Morris does extensive work with this in his book *Irreverent Acting,* from which these two exercises come. I refer you to that book for more examples.

Stream-of-consciousness exercises make the actor aware of the multitude of stimuli that bombard him from moment to moment. They may be sensory in nature, or they may be feelings and attitudes caused by a person, place, or object. The key to these exercises is to acknowledge the stimuli and speak aloud about how they affect you. The exercises are done privately but semiaudibly, as addressing the stimuli verbally affords them importance. We find we cannot brush them aside as we do mentally.

The exercises are not easy, and students will often say that they cannot "stay in the present." The difficulty here is one of truly understanding the objective of the exercise. The actor is not asked to "perform"; he is asked to be truthful to himself. If I feel that a class is tense prior to this activity, I will lead them through some basic warm-ups to relax them.

I feel that these stream-of-consciousness exercises are very beneficial for the actor. When he becomes more comfortable with living "in the present" he can more easily make his stage work appear fresh and unrehearsed.

Materials:

Procedure:

Part I:

Introduce the concept of the stream-of-consciousness. Explain that time is broken into three parts—past, present, and future. Of the three, the present is the most difficult to deal with because it is the most fleeting. While words come out of the mouth, they become part of the past. Time may be compared to sitting on a train and looking out the window. The scenery passes quickly. Actors, however, must train themselves to stay in the present.

Do a stream-of-consciousness exercise for the class. Sit before them, preferably on the floor, and have the class sit with you. Relax a bit before starting.

Speak aloud as you note elements in your environment as they occur. "Right now I am sitting on the floor with all of you near me. I'm conscious of the fact that you are looking at me, and this makes me a bit uptight. I can hear voices in the hallway outside the room. There is a fly buzzing around my right hand. My back is bothering me," etc.

The thoughts may be disjointed, and you may interrupt yourself as you are bombarded by different stimuli in the environment. But this is often the case with stream-of-consciousness work.

Ask students if they have any questions. If not, tell them they may go anywhere in the space they choose. They may sit, stand, or lie down. They should be comfortable. Stress the importance of speaking aloud. We speak more slowly than we think, and speaking our thoughts makes us focus on them more strongly.

After a few minutes ask the students to return and share their reactions. Did they find it difficult to remain in the present? Did they become more aware of stimuli in the environment? How does this relate to acting? One important point to make is that acting should appear as if it were occurring for the first time; that the character be totally engaged in the present no matter how much rehearsal has gone into that moment on the stage. This exercise emphasizes the sensation of staying in the present. Students often claim that they run our of things to say, and must be reminded that they should not be "inventing" but rather *responding* to stimuli in the environment.

Part II:

The next step is to do the "How Do I Feel?" Exercise. This is similar to the Stream-of-Consciousness, and you should demonstrate this one also. Repeat the phrase "How do I feel?" throughout the exercise.

How do I feel? Right now I feel a bit anxious because everyone is watching me. How do I feel? Melancholy because I had to bring my only child to college recently and I miss her terribly. I know most people don't consider it a big deal, but I feel both excited for her and sad too. How do I feel? Pressured because I don't have a break between classes, so I must plan all my lessons and have all materials ready long before I get to class. How do I feel? Cold. The heat is off in the building. My back has been bothering me since I started this new exercise in the morning, etc.

If there are no questions, repeat the procedure used for the Stream-of-Consciousness. Students may go wherever they want to do the exercise. Again, they must speak aloud, but not loud enough for anyone else to hear them. They should have privacy to deal honestly with their feelings.

Have the students return for discussion after completing the exercise. Did they like it? Did they learn something new about themselves that they didn't know before the exercise? How does this relate to acting?

Students usually react extremely well to this exercise, and often discover reasons for their feelings, etc. It's quite self-revelatory, and they often like to do this exercise at home.

Part III:

You may want to do a "cool-down" theater game if time permits. The exercises we have been doing thus far in this class, while relaxing, need to be balanced with some high activity, "fun" cool-downs. I suggest "Donkey, Rabbit" in Lesson 22 of Introduction to Acting, Part I of this book.

Objectives:

The student will:
- learn the importance of the stream-of-consciousness in acting
- focus on stimuli in the immediate environment
- recognize feelings he is experiencing
- grow in self-awareness
- share ideas

And in the theater game "Donkey, Rabbit":
- think quickly
- learn sequential tasks
- use the body in space
- memorize gestures in relation to "trigger" commands

Lessons 13–14
Psychophysical (Dramatic) Scene Study

Commentary
See the commentary for Lessons 14–15 in Part I: Introduction to Acting.

Lesson 13

Preparing for the Dramatic Scene

Materials:
preselected psychophysical (dramatic) scenes
Scenework Progress Charts
(These are in Part III, Scene Study)

Procedure:

Part I:
Remind students of the scenes they performed in the Introductory Course. Allow them to talk about their feelings toward the scenes, their effort, etc. What did they learn from that project? What would they do differently if they had to do the same scene over again?

The Advanced Course includes two scene study experiences rather than one: one psychophysical (or dramatic) scene, and one comedy scene. Today we will begin the psychophysical scene.

Explain that the scenes have been carefully chosen to develop the potential of each member of the class.

While future lessons will deal with specific aspects of psychophysical acting, today we will merely become acquainted with the scene. Ask students to meet with their scene study partners in a comfortable and private part of the theater to read the scene aloud. Explain that you will travel to each group to answer any questions or clear up any problems they may have.

Remind students of the Scenework Progress Charts which must be filled out for every rehearsal. Give each group a copy today. (See Part III, Scene Study, for charts).

Part II:
Pass out the scene to the actors. They may now move to a part of the theater to read the scene. Collect the progress charts at the end of the period.

Objectives:
The student will:
- be made aware of expectations of the Scene Study Unit
- become familiar with the preselected scene and partner

Lesson 14
Performing the Dramatic Scene

Materials:
Actors in the scene being presented will bring in their own props, costumes, etc. The class will need copies of the Scene Evaluation Form from Part III, Scene Study.

Procedure:
Several classes will now be devoted to the performance of the psychophysical scenes currently being worked on. The chapter on scene study provides detailed instructions for the post-performance critique.

As the actors prepare to perform, give the class the necessary information (name of the scene, playwright, actors' and characters' names, etc.).

Tell the class to take brief notes on the back of the evaluation sheet during the scene. Students do not want to take so many notes that they miss a substantial part of the performance.

The scene is performed and videotaped.

At the completion of the scene, the actors discuss the Script Analysis Chart, telling what the scene is about ("This is the story of what happens when . . ."), the characters' objectives, and the climax.

The next step is the Post-Performance Critique (see this section in the Scene Study Unit).

The instructor works with the actors to correct major acting problems in the scene.

The Scene Evaluation Forms are completed as homework, handed in the next class, and given to the actors. This provides feedback from colleagues.

Obviously, the steps described may take more than one class period. The teacher must determine the amount of time needed to devote to each scene.

Objectives:
The student will:
- perform a psychophysical (dramatic) scene from a play (includes costumes, props, set, etc.)
- critique the scene according to proper procedure
- complete the Scene Evaluation Form
- analyze the scene from a literary/performance point of view
- correct acting problems through teacher coaching
- apply lesson to his own acting problems

Lessons 15–17
Subtext, the Essence of Acting

Commentary

Subtext is often a confusing term. When dealing with a specific script, subtext is just that—the meaning which lies "under the text." It is thought of as the actor speaks the line and, therefore, is extremely helpful in that it supplies motivation. Needless to say, it affects the manner in which the line of dialogue is spoken.

Stanislavsky felt that subtext was of enormous importance to an actor, that it provided a rich depth of meaning which colored the actor's words with truth and believability. Homework was essential, then, as actors supplied background information—often yielded by the text, often implied, and often created by the actor's imagination—so that every line was justified and firmly based in truth. The actor must explore the play and himself.

When actors create subtext outside the script material, they obviously draw from their storehouse of "inner resources"—books they have read, places they have visited, people they have known, sensory experiences they have had, etc. The subtext becomes a process of substituting the real for the imaginary, the actor's real experiences for the character's fictional ones. This substitution may take the form of endowing stage properties with the characteristics of "the real thing"; it may take the form of recalling sensory experiences; and it may require the recollection of emotional moments as well.

Furthermore, subtext can have a more general definition for the director. It could represent the "meaning" of the text which, while nowhere specified, can determine the interpretation of the play and the director's approach to it. It would have a definite impact on the way an actor prepares for the play and his role. Subtext, therefore, has a broad meaning, ranging from the director's interpretation of the play to simple textual allusions to major emotional memories—all geared to making the actor's performance believable.

Both the subtext assignments in Lesson 13 are from classical dramatic literature, and both deal with highly emotional moments. Perhaps the lesson, in addition to dealing with this all-important aspect of acting, will spur students to read some classical plays as well, as a familiarity with these, I believe, is imperative for the well-trained actor. I feel that training in the classics is invaluable, and that performing in contemporary plays is easier when an actor is rooted in such training.

Actors may ask about the depth of the emotion in the selected model assignments and how they can possibly find adequate emotional subtext. Indeed, when I was directing *Othello,* my Othello asked me just that: "How do you find subtext/motivation for strangling someone?" The post-performance discussion is important for sharing possible methods of finding such subtext. Often the events of the play—the textual subtext—can supply the motivation. Iago, after all, is cruel and manipulative. However, I feel the connections to the emotional subtext needed are also very possible. We all feel jealousy. It is, as Iago says, "that green-eyed monster" which can make us do some pretty dreadful things in the name of revenge. Some of these situations should be explored and offered as possible solutions.

The emotional-subtext assignment ties the study of subtext to our stream-of-consciousness work in Lesson 12. Students select one of the given situations and prepare to perform it for the class. They may sit or stand, whichever is more comfortable, and speak as the character, firmly rooted in the present. While some of the situations may be identifiable for some actors, others definitely will not be. Class discussion, after commenting on the strong points of the performance, should focus on a process of finding appropriate subtext for use in playing these characters. Its value is obvious in that actors must often play characters very different from themselves.

A final word: Subtext requires homework, either textual—and that involves not only the plot and character but often research of historical events, manners, clothing, costumes, etc.—and emotional. Without subtext, acting is flat, one-dimensional, and artificial; it's what joins the actor and the role, allowing the creation of a vital character.

Lesson 15
Defining Subtext

Materials:
Emotional Subtext Assignment Sheet (following this lesson)

Procedure:
Today's lesson will deal with subtext.

The class should begin with a definition of subtext. If class members cannot define it, the teacher should. Subtext is rather complex (see the Commentary on this lesson). It can relate to specific textual references regarding events or people with whom a certain character should be familiar. It may also include feelings and thoughts that the actor experiences while delivering specific lines of dialogue. Personal subtext will differ among actors, for subtext is found within the individual when dealing with thoughts and feelings. It comes from the actor's experiences in life. Therefore, while the outer appearances of two actors' respective performances of a given role may be somewhat similar, the internal imagery and motivations may be very different.

Ask for one female and one male volunteer to perform the following subtext situations. Explain the circumstances to each actor privately. Each will then perform.

For the female volunteer: Sophocles' *Antigone* draws a picture of Antigone, a strong-willed and defiant young woman. Her brother, Polyneices, was declared a traitor by Creon, the ruler of the kingdom. His body, therefore, is denied proper burial and is left to rot on the battlefield. Antigone defies the order. She pours three libations on the corpse to sanctify it and then proceeds to cover the body with large amounts of dust. She had done this previously, but members of the army had uncovered it. She is therefore angry as she performs this activity. She says aloud, "How can I not be loyal to my family?" as she works.

After the performance, commend the actress for the effective moments. Ask the class what they feel was happening in this scene. Discuss not only the plot, but also the manner in which the actions were carried out. Ask the students what they think the spoken line meant in relation to the action.

After the discussion, supply the subtext given above. You may then deal with the emotional part of the performance. What can any actor use for subtext in this situation? Is having a sibling wronged in some way enough? Students may share some personal history or experiences for possible use, but that is not really the most important thing here. General suggestions for emotional subtext and how to go about finding the subtext is perhaps *more* valuable—especially since the situation is so "distant" from the usual course of our lives.

Have the male volunteer perform the following activity from Shakespeare's *Othello*.

Othello is an army general who has been duped by the cunning, evil Iago, Othello's companion and an army officer, into thinking that Desdemona, Othello's wife, has been unfaithful. Iago convinces Othello that Desdemona has been having an affair with Cassio, an army officer whom Othello promoted in place of Iago (a possible motive for Iago's revenge). After much thought, and "proof" supplied by Iago, Othello determines that he must kill his unfaithful wife. Late at night, he steals into her bedroom where she lies asleep. Othello carries a candle, as the room is dark. He moves to the bed, looking down at the sleeping woman, gazing at her beauty and seeming innocence. The spoken line is, "She must die, else she'll betray more men." Othello then strangles her.

Follow the same format for the post-performance discussion described above.

Hand out the Subtext Assignment Sheet which follows this lesson. It is important to note that this is a difficult assignment and should be explained with utmost clarity. It is the actor's task to select one of the given situations, create the character and the circumstance, and act it out for the class. These situations differ from other improvisations in that they are highly charged emotionally and force the actor to make subtextual connections if they are to be performed believably.

Some of the situations will be easy for the student actors to identify with. They may have experienced them, or perhaps their friends have (although there is often great courage called for when acting out a circumstance that hits home). Other situations will be more difficult and will therefore present a challenge much like that faced by any professional actor. He must try to understand the character and his feelings, and subsequently create a believable performance, drawing from the "inner resources" of his own life—his own experiences, his readings, the places he's traveled, the people he's known, the movies he's seen, etc. This will facilitate an understanding of the character's situation from the actor's perspective. In other words, he is searching for connections between his own experience and that of the character. He is supplying subtext for a truthful delivery of lines and a believable creation of character.

However, the jump from one's feelings of anger over being swindled in the purchase of a used car to Othello's rage over his wife's supposed infidelity is quite another story, and certainly a good topic for discussion. When asked about the extreme difference in circumstances, I respond that the answer lies in the *essence* of the emotion. I have often compared the grief experienced by an adult over the death of a loved one to that of my then nine-year-old brother when he saw his cat lying dead in the street. No one could have convinced that grief-stricken child that any situation could be worse. Certainly age exposes us to a host of more complex and sophisticated problems, but for purposes of training an actor of any age, we need to examine the intensity of the emotion itself rather than the situation.

When the student selects one of the choices, he must become *actively involved* in communicating the actions and objective. In choice 2, for example, the daughter might tell her parents at the dinner table, or she may burst into the house after having the pregnancy confirmed at the doctor's office. In choice 8 the location might be a drive-in movie or a confrontation between classes at school.

Finding the appropriate subtext for use in emotional situations is central to the training of an actor. After the exercise, the class should discuss the believability of the performance. Ask students what inner resources would help with a truthful character identification. Ask if there are any students who feel they cannot relate to the situation at all. What subtext choices, then, might be explored? Discuss all possibilities.

Objectives:
The student will:
- learn the meaning of subtext in textual, sensory, and emotional terms
- explore subtextual options through sample performance situations
- search within himself to "connect" with a subtext assignment

Emotional Subtext Assignment Sheet

Each student actor should select one of the following situations and relate his feelings, as if he were the character, to the class:

1. You have just placed your elderly parent, who is suffering from Alzheimer's Disease, in a rest home. How do you feel?

2. A daughter must tell her parents that she is pregnant. You may perform the role of the daughter or one of the parents.

3. Against your father's instructions, you took his new car for a ride when he was away for the weekend. As you were pulling into the garage, a jutting piece of metal made a deep scratch along the entire length of the car. Tell your father what happened.

4. You are Jewish and a new student at a large public high school. When you return to your locker at the end of the day, you find a large swastika scrawled on it. How do you feel? Tell the principal or your parents.

5. Your sister's husband is an alcoholic, and you must tell your sister that he has been secretly stealing money from relatives to support his drinking problem. Speak as if you are breaking the news to your sister.

6. You forgot to respond to your friend's wedding invitation, and today, the day of the wedding, you receive an irate phone call from the bride telling you that you are inconsiderate and have cost her money for the reception meal by not responding. Speak to the bride as if you were receiving the phone call.

7. A teenager "comes out" to his parents, telling them that he or she is gay. You may perform as the teenager or the parent.

8. A member of the opposite sex tells you that he or she loves you, but you do not feel the same about that person. Tell him or her.

9. A teenager feels seriously neglected by his parents. They are always away on business or at work, leaving the only child home alone nearly all of the time. Tell this as if you were the teenager speaking to your parent(s).

10. You have fallen in love and decided to marry a person of a different race. You must tell your parents, who you know are bigots.

11. You are walking through the woods in the evening after a snowfall. The full moon lights your way. Describe this scene of natural beauty.

12. A superior at work has made sexual innuendos to you. You desperately need this job but are genuinely upset by the callow remarks, gestures, and proposals of your boss. Tell him or her.

13. You have witnessed a crime of some magnitude and can identify the guilty party. Supply the circumstances and then tell the guilty party what you have witnessed and what you intend to do.

14. You are walking home with your much younger brother during a terrible snowstorm. The snow is accumulating at an extremely fast rate. You have decided to take a shortcut through a lot containing houses under construction, many of which have foundations only, and no walls. Suddenly, you cannot find your brother and fear that he has fallen through the snow into the basement of one of the unfinished homes. Tell this as if it were a phone conversation with your parents.

Lesson 16
Performing the Subtext Assignment

Materials:
brought in by students for the performance of their subtext assignments

Procedure:
This lesson will provide the format for the performance of the subtext assignments given in Lesson 15. This design may be used for all classes devoted to this assignment.

The number of students to perform today is predetermined, and they are scheduled approximately two or three days in advance.

Part I:
The class, including the performers, should relax before presentations. This can be achieved through one or two deep breaths. While their eyes are closed and after the deep breath is taken, the teacher should ask the class to perform a stream-of-consciousness exercise (see Lesson 12) for just a moment. Follow this with another deep breath. The class should now be ready for the first presentation.

Part II:
The actor performs his subtext assignment.

The class and teacher critique the performance. Use, as always, the proper procedure for all oral critiques.

While the teacher must lead all post-performance critiques, he should also use his own skills in training an actor. As each actor is very different, so must the acting teacher work with each student in a specific and unique way. If the acting teacher has done his "homework" and has gotten to "know" each student's abilities as much as possible, this work session will be facilitated. You may want to change the circumstances or setting; you may want to use different methods to evoke qualities the actor was not aware of. This work session develops the actor and provides a learning experience for the class.

Objectives:
The student will:
- use subtext in acting
- learn the relationship between subtext and psychophysical acting
- become more self-aware through the work session
- observe the work session and apply the concepts to his own development

Lesson 17

An Emotional Improvisation

Materials:
copy of a letter from a son to his parents (following this lesson)

Procedure:
This improvisation, which is strong in emotional value, is an appropriate follow-up to the individual subtext performances. This performance uses three actors. The improvisational situation is very dynamic and deals with the real problem of socially morally "correct" choices versus one's true feelings. The circumstance is provided by James Duff's play *Home Front* and concerns a son's request to bring a friend, severely hurt in the war, home to live with the family.

You may find the post-performance discussion as exciting as the improvisation itself. Allow everyone an opportunity to express his feelings. You may deal with such things as the difference between intellectual justification and truthful emotional responses, as well as Jimmy's relationship to the man who saved his life.

For closure to this lesson, remind students that, as this lesson proves, they are capable of very strong feelings, and that they should learn to be aware—almost in a detached way—of these feelings when they occur, and continually build up their storehouse of inner resources for future use.

Ask for three volunteers to do the improvisation. Both sexes should be represented.

The characters are a husband, wife, and teenage daughter or son. The set is the living room of their home. Tell the class that the family has just received a letter from their son Jimmy, who has been away fighting in the war. Give the letter to either parent, who is reading it as he or she enters the living room after having gotten the mail.

Allow the improvisation to come to its end, which is when an answer to Jimmy's question is decided upon.

Ask the actors if they feel comfortable as characters with the solution they have come up with. Then ask them if their own feelings would have been different.

Encourage the class members to offer their opinions. They may at first say that Jimmy would be more than welcome to bring his handicapped friend to their homes. Ask them to examine their true feelings. Would they really want the responsibility of caring for Jimmy's friend?

Would it be a temporary stay or a permanent one? What would they feel comfortable with?

Tell the students the actual end of this true story, that a while after the parents responded to Jimmy's letter saying that their son could bring home his friend temporarily, they received a telegram from the commanding officer telling them that Jimmy had committed suicide. Jimmy had no friend. It was *he* who, in fact, had his body torn apart by a bomb. He wanted to "test" his parents' ability to deal with this ordeal.

Encourage students to express their opinions about Jimmy's actions. Some will say it was a generous thing he did for his parents, while some will say it was a terrible thing.

In connecting this experience with acting training, tell the students that they are continuing to deal with their feelings and, in the process, becoming more self-aware. If they emphasized the circumstances of the "life-saving act" as mentioned above, explain the relationship between their need for this information and the character's/actor's need for knowledge about the circumstances surrounding an action or decision.

Objectives:
The student will:
- continue to become more self-aware
- deal with true feelings rather than socially "nice" ones
- learn that circumstances influence decision-making
- interpret written material

A Letter from Jimmy

Dear Mom and Dad,

I will be home very shortly and would like your permission to bring home a friend to live with us. He saved my life. He lost both his legs and one arm in an explosion. Please discuss this and let me know what your answer is. He saved my life.

Love,
Your son,
Jimmy

Lesson 18

The Detonation Exercise

Commentary

Maxine Klein's book *Time, Space, and Designs for Actors* is the source of this most powerful "Detonation" exercise. During the exercise, student actors experience powerful emotions after going through a sensory buildup of real or imaginary circumstances. The many positive elements of this exercise include the surfacing—often to the surprise of the participants—of very real and very potent emotions, the release of many pent-up frustrations, and a nearly "guaranteed" success in providing a sense of accomplishment for the actor.

You do not want to run out of time during this exercise. If this occurs, you will release some very tense and volatile people into the community. Plan your time wisely. Work at a leisurely pace so that the exercise is not rushed. Use your voice to guide and control the feelings your actors may be experiencing.

The objective of this exercise, as with numerous others, is to help the actor learn to concentrate, which in turn permits a flow of feelings which have been suppressed through years of environmental conditioning. One of the important responsibilities of the acting teacher is to create conditions of privacy and a nonjudgmental atmosphere where the actor can feel free to experiment, explore, and often "fall flat on his face."

In truth, there is no way for the acting teacher to know whether the Detonation Exercise is successful from observing his students' involvement. The emotional experience is "invisible," other than hearing the spoken line which culminates the exercise. It is hoped that by this stage of development in the training program, the sensory aspect of the Detonation Exercise will enable the release of strong emotion.

But it is important that the teacher not pressure the student into claiming that valid emotion was indeed felt during this or any other private exercise. "Demanding" success, or judging one's own teaching competencies by the students' mastery of any assignment, is detrimental to building an atmosphere of trust and freedom. The Detonation Exercise, as any other, may be performed several times during the course.

Materials:

Procedure:

This exercise, the Detonation, is used with the psychophysical scene study of Part III of this book and deals with "getting in touch" with one's feelings and being able to express them.

Part I:

Relax the class through a series of exercises (centering, spine fold, head roll, some deep breaths).

Part II:

Ask the students to spread out throughout the space. Each should "claim" a spot of his own, finding objects (a piece of furniture, a mark on the floor, etc.) to define that space. The students should feel comfortable in their respective spaces and should assume a comfortable position. Tell them that they can see out of the space, but no one can see into it. This will give each student a feeling of privacy.

Today we will deal with the line "Who do you think you are!"

Ask students to think about a time when they actually said this to someone, or a time when they wished they had said this.

After a few moments, lead the students through a sensory recall of the environment in which the experience occurred. Tell them *not* to think of the person involved, or even the situation. We will first think only of the setting.

Deal with the sense of sight. Speak slowly, giving ample time for the students to follow your directions. Your goal is to encourage them to *see* the space, whether indoors or out, as acutely as possible. Deal with colors, sizes, shapes, detail. Tell them to notice one thing that they never noticed before.

Move on to the sense of hearing. Again, encourage detail. Ask them to hear one thing they never heard before.

Do the same with touch, smell, and taste. This last sense is perhaps the most difficult to do in this context. Most environments do not have food, but perhaps they could taste a flower, or imagine the taste of that imposing, dark mahogany desk. Synesthesia occurs here, when a stimulus of one type produces a subjective sensation. For example, the smell of the flower produces an accompanying taste sensation.

The next step is to introduce the person to whom the actor will say "Who do you think you are!" The situation still has not been introduced.

Remind the students that they are invisible and therefore may get as close to the person as they wish. Slowly walk around the person. What is his/her size? Color? Color of clothing? Notice the hair. Are there streaks of gray? Notice one thing about this person you never noticed before. Also, how does this person smell? Is it cologne, perfume, hairspray, natural odor?

Now introduce the situation. Tell the students that they should think of the situation in detail. They may not, however, speak the line "Who do you think you are!" until they have earned the right to say it. This can only be achieved through a total commitment to the situation and line. They must say it aloud any way they feel they should.

Part III:

After all of the students have spoken the line, gather them around to talk about the experience. If the exercise has worked, the results will be astonishing. Many will not have thought they "had it in them." Some will not believe the intensity of their feelings. Many will feel good about having said the line.

Extension:

Try other lines, such as "I love you," "I hate you," "It's beautiful," etc.

Objectives:

The student will:
- relax mentally and physically
- become more self-aware
- explore specific feelings
- express himself emotionally
- share results and feelings with his classmates
- learn the importance of subtext in acting

Lessons 19–20
Dealing with Emotion

Commentary

These lessons are carefully placed in the sequence of those dealing with emotions and their use on the stage, the ultimate goal of which is to prepare student actors to handle those often difficult, yet richly rewarding, dramatic moments. The performance assignment in Lesson 19 concerns four major emotions: love, anger, fear, and grief. People of all ages have fairly extensive experiences in at least one of these.

Students should be carefully guided in preparing this performance assignment, and two areas need special attention:

The plot should be well-developed. There must be a beginning, middle, and end, with transitions smoothly flowing from one to the other. Some student actors tend to get so concerned with the emotion that the plot becomes flimsy and uninteresting. Also, challenge the students to be unique in this area. I cannot tell you how many student actors play baby-sitters who, alone with a sleeping child, hear noises in the next room!

When the piece is performed, you may offer suggestions for the expansion and development of these "episodes" into more fully fleshed-out plots. Again, as with all individual performance assignments, the actor is working alone but should feel free to relate to important yet "invisible" characters.

Substitutions (emotional subtext) should not be shared. When actors reveal their substitutions, especially in terms of emotional subtext, they tend to lose their potency. Perhaps it is merely a matter of someone in the audience knowing the actor's "secrets." Also, subtext is much too personal to share; the actor's privacy should be protected.

Tell the actor not to use something traumatic for subtext if it occurred within the last three years. Some teachers feel even three years is too short a period of time, because its recollection could trigger an emotional breakdown on stage—especially if the actor has not really dealt with that experience yet. If it happens, comfort the actor. Make sure, however, that the class learns why this breakdown occurred, as it is a good lesson for actors.

A special note: There are many words in the teaching of acting that seem to mean the same thing, or to be so closely related that they seem to mean the same thing: subtext, substitution, emotional subtext, endowment, emotional recall, sensory recall. In the final analysis, it does not really matter what the words are. The main idea is that the best acting draws upon the actor's personal life—the people he knows, the places he's been, the experiences he's had, the emotions he's felt, the flowers he's smelled, the sunrises he's seen on the way to work, the sound of the dentist's drill in the other room, the embarrassing moments, the successes and failures, and so on. It all adds up to a lot of homework—and a very sensitized, observant human being.

Lesson 19
Substituting an Emotion

Materials:
none

Procedure:
Begin class today by reviewing subtext in its different forms. Trace the evolution of our work with emotions from the individual emotional subtext assignments to the improvisation about Jimmy in Lesson 17 to the most recent work with emotional detonations.

When we work in this area we are actually substituting our own emotions for those of the character. But we constantly substitute when we act, and not only emotionally. We substitute for every element in the text: we substitute one person for another; we endow props with the qualities of real objects (see Introductory Course, Lesson 13); and we use sense memory substitutions dealing with sight, touch, taste, smell, and hearing.

Now we will delve even further into our emotions for use on stage. Students must choose among the emotions of love, anger, fear, and grief and create a fictional set of circumstances during which the chosen emotion is evoked. The emotion will be real, drawing upon events, people, or experiences in the actor's life. The actor must then perform the circumstances for the class.

Warn the student actors that the situation must have a solid plot, with a beginning, middle, and end.

This situation is very similar to that found in any given play: The plot is fictional, but the emotion is truthful because the actor taps into some event in his life that elicits that emotion. This will require the actor to substitute, or use what Stanislavsky called "emotional recall."

Assign the Emotional Recall performances as defined above and set a performance date. I usually give a week for preparation of this assignment.

Objectives:
The student will:
- learn to define substitution
- learn that there are many kinds of substitutions, one of which is emotional recall
- prepare a performance in which he will use truthful emotions in a fictional situation

Lesson 20

Performing the Emotional Recall Assignment

Materials:
brought in by students for the performance of the Emotional Recall assignment

Procedure:
Specific students have been assigned today as their performance day. If this is the first of such performance days, it might be a good idea to review the assignment as a means of highlighting what students will see today—a fictional situation in which the actor experiences a real emotion (love, anger, fear, or grief).

I require my students to keep an acting notebook in which to take notes on relevant points of class discussion, and also to note aspects of another actor's work. It is important to tell students *not* to spend time writing during a performance, for the obvious reason that they will miss most of it. These notes may be made after the performance.

The student performs the assignment.

The post-performance critique should begin with the question "What did you see?" Lead the class to an objective observation of the work. Include the set, perhaps the selection of costume (or suggested costume), and the plot of the presentation. This segment of the critique is non-evaluative. You may ask questions like "How did the costume colors affect you?" "What was this story about?"

The actor may then say whether these were intended effects.

The "judgmental" part of the critique must be handled with tact. You might begin with "What did you like about this performance?" "Did it move you?" and gradually lead up to "What were some other options for achieving this effect?" Encourage the students to explore possibilities.

The teacher should take one or two areas that need attention and use his skills to help the student improve. I find it is better to work this way rather than list 140 things "wrong" with the performance. The student can work on one or two major problems now. Other problems will not disappear and can be addressed with future assignments.

Objectives:
The student will:
- learn to critique the performances of others
- create a fictional situation
- create a real emotion in a fictional situation
- create a character through body movement and voice
- design a simple set
- select appropriate, suggestive costumes

Lessons 21–23
Preparing Scenes

Commentary

These lessons are important while student actors are preparing their respective scenes. They deal with more complex aspects of scene preparation and character development than most actors in the Introductory Course are ready to explore. All are intended to make the actor more closely analyze the conditions of the text, and become more familiar with the character.

Many actors feel that a character's life exists only on the stage. While this may be "factually" true, it is both pragmatic and advantageous to think about what the character would be doing *prior* to the scene, for this obviously determines his attitude when the audience first sees him. Likewise, events of the scene affect what happens to the character *afterward*. The sense of pre- and post-scene, then, reaffirms the existence of a character's life when not seen by the audience, and by doing so adds believability, humanity, and depth to the role.

Another point to consider is that the pre-scene events also affect the way actors conceive beats in the onstage scene. Where the character is coming from prior to the scene affects timing and the way dramatic tensions are created on stage. A good example of this is the climactic scene with Nina and Treplev in *The Seagull*. Nina enters after lurking about in the garden. She is anxiety-ridden and distracted, and Treplev cannot soothe her despite his protestations of love.

The tensions may even be greater if several characters are brought together, each with a different sense of pre-scene, as is the case in *King Lear* where so much of the play depends on the pre-Act I, scene i actions and emotions of Lear and his three daughters. An interesting point in this regard concerns O'Neill's original set design for *Desire Under the Elms,* which calls for a façade of a farmhouse with the front wall cut away, thus exposing the rooms of the two-level house simultaneously. Characters not involved in the main action in the kitchen may still be seen going about their business in other parts of the house. This poses an interesting twist to pre- and post-scene awareness, as the audience can actually see much of this activity. Obviously, there are moments when the characters are offstage and cannot be seen.

Parts of an Action/Assimilation (Lesson 22) is one I find of great value in slowing the actor down and making him truly analyze the character's thought process and resulting physical action. Many acting teachers have their own ideas pertaining to the number of steps in an action and the corresponding names of those steps. I personally prefer Robert L. Benedetti's analysis in *The Actor at Work*. Again, these variations are not as important as the realization that stage life includes more than mere action-reaction responses, that there are intermediary steps, and those steps are important.

I stress assimilation a great deal, because I find that to be a moment of vulnerability and one which captivates the audience. As such, it is powerful and engaging. Assimilation is critically important because it is the moment between the external stimulus and the response, between the phenomenon and the reaction. It is the moment of fundamental *internal* action. The visible response must be connected in some way to this moment, or any subsequent action loses its credibility. In daily life the moment of assimilation is rarely seen, but in the theater we *do* see this moment, making an acting performance special, precious, and even profound. The teacher should be prepared to offer another example or two of an action and its parts in addition to the one provided in this lesson. Another factor to emphasize is that actions are continuous. One ends and another begins immediately as characters—and all of us as well—are continually bombarded with stimuli in our world.

Lesson 23 deals with body control centers, a lesson inspired by Maxine Klein. This lesson will encourage actors to explore body language (first introduced in the Introductory Course, Lesson 4) and movement in developing characterization, possibly opening doors to the character's physicality that had not been thought of previously.

Lesson 21

Pre- and Post-Scene Awareness

Materials:
none

Procedure:
The focus of today's lesson is on conveying a sense of pre-scene and post-scene.

Part I:
Begin class with a brief warm-up exercise. Select a theater game from Lesson 22 in the Introductory Course, Part I of this book.

Part II:
Explain to the students the necessity of a pre- and post-scene life for the characters they are presently working on in their scene-study unit.

All too often, characters are "alive" onstage only for the duration of the scene. A concept which should be introduced to actors on the advanced level is the creation of a life for the character prior to what we, the audience, actually see of him, as well as after. "Where is this character coming from just before the scene (or play) begins?" "How did he feel when he was there?" "Where will the character go when this scene or play ends?" The answers to these questions will help us "flesh out" the character and make him more realistic or believable.

Today we will do a pre- and post-scene exercise.

The actor must imagine three settings side-by-side in the front of the playing space. The class will be able to see only the center setting. The actor must enter the center setting from the first setting. His objective is to tell the class where he came from through his actions only. The actor should perform some simple activity in the middle setting, and then, again through his actions only, communicate where he is going (the third setting).

An example of this is:

The actor enters hurriedly brushing his teeth (coming from the bathroom—first setting) to the living room. He looks out the window to see if his ride has arrived. He puts the toothbrush down on a table, goes to a closet and chooses from among several jackets to wear. He puts on sneakers, the selected jacket, and takes a basket-

ball from the closet. He "hears" a car horn and exits (to his friend in the car—third setting).

Give students some time to disperse throughout the space and rehearse an exercise of their own. Much of this will obviously be pantomime.

Call students back and begin presentations.

Objectives:

The student will:

- learn to create a more realistic character through pre- and post-scene awareness
- create a pre- and post-scene exercise
- interpret others' exercises using given information to determine pre- and post-scene settings

Lesson 22
The Parts of an Action/Assimilation

I feel that this lesson is an extremely important one, and it can often make the difference between mediocre and truly fine acting. I include it in the Advanced Course, but it should be addressed in the Introductory Course as well. It should be part of all critiques of scenes and other acting projects. In fact, assimilation should be a common word in the actor's vocabulary.

Materials:
scenes that students are currently working on

Procedure:

Part I:
It is difficult to determine how or when a discussion of assimilation and the parts of an action may arise. Obviously, whether it stands as a lesson on its own or whether it arises as an element of a class critique will determine the first step in procedure.

Tell students that any action has six parts:

- stimulus
- assimilation
- decision pertaining to possible responses
- planning to respond
- response
- evaluation of response.

At this point, an example of the above would be helpful. I have used the following:

A person is waiting for a phone call with some trepidation, for the phone call deals with the health of a close friend after surgery.

The phone rings. This is the *stimulus.* The person "takes in" the fact that the phone is ringing, and many thoughts run through his mind. Has his friend pulled through the operation? Has his condition worsened? Did he survive? This is the *assimilation.*

Decisions pertaining to his response to the ringing phone are now thought of.

Should he answer the phone? Should he ignore it? Should he call someone else to answer it? He makes a *decision* to answer the phone.

The *planning* in this case is rather simple. He approaches the phone. He picks up the phone. This is the *response.*

The *evaluation* of the response is quick. He may feel good that he has answered the phone, because this response will now force him to receive the news, whether it is good or bad. At least the decision is over.

Notice that the completion of this action initiates the next action. The actor must now assimilate the news at the other end of the phone.

In discussing this example, inform students that the part of the action most often missing in performance by inexperienced actors is the assimilation. Very often actors betray the fact that they already know the fate of the patient, because they know the script. The response is therefore artificial and planned.

One of the most exciting parts of a live performance is to see and understand how the characters assimilate information.

Ask the class if there are any questions. You may need to give another step-by-step example.

Part II:

The class should now break down into performance groups according to the scenes they are currently working on. They should examine the scene and discuss one specific action, "talking through" the moment of assimilation.

Objectives:

The student will:
- learn the six parts of an action
- learn the importance of assimilation
- find examples of the six parts of an action in his current acting project

Lesson 23

Body Control Centers

Materials:
none

Procedure:
Tell student actors that the subject of today's lesson is body control centers.

Part I:
Begin class with some exercises. A spine fold and head roll can relax students quickly and effectively.

Ask students to close their eyes, spread their legs slightly, and try to imagine themselves equally as heavy on the right side of the body as on the left, with the spine in direct center.

Now tell them to make the right side slightly heavier, then even more so. Do the same with the left side. Ask them to slowly shift weight from one side to the other, acknowledging when they are "centered" but not stopping the movement.

Part II:
Ask students if they can define "body language." Then give some examples, ranging from those demonstrated by people who seem very "loose," with flailing arms and large, bouncy steps, to others who seem "tight," with arms and legs tense or crossed, always placing objects, like barriers, between themselves and others. Still others seem almost ethereal in their movements, light and airy, almost like floating as they move.

Actors can learn a great deal through observation of body language, which is a physical manifestation of a person's self-concept, attitudes, thoughts, feelings, fears, how they want to be perceived, etc.

Imagine that there are control centers in various areas of the body that determine how we think and, subsequently, how we move, act, and behave. One control center dominates the others. Where do you think your dominating control center is?

Is it in the brain or head?

Are you always deep in thought, studious, philosophical, pondering, inquisitive, curious?

Is it in the heart?

Are you always concerned about others, more so than yourself? Are you sensitive, sacrificial, nurturing, caring, maternal, paternal, loving, passionate?

Is it in the stomach?

Are you nervous about many things? Do you always see the worst possible outcome? Are you afraid of failure? Do you have "butterflies" before an important engagement? Are you frequently in conflict with others? with yourself? Are you angry? frustrated?

Is it in the groin?

Are your looks extremely important to you? Is it important to build up your body? Do you enjoy stylish, yet suggestive clothing? Is sex important to you? Sensuality? Being attractive to others?

Students should walk throughout the space, exploring the movement dictated by a particular body control center. All energy should emanate from that center so that it is the source of power and control. The teacher should call these control centers aloud, giving sufficient time for this exploration. Students should work individually so that they feel free to express themselves physically.

After students have had enough time to explore all of the centers, ask which control centers felt most comfortable and which felt the least comfortable. Many questions will surface, such as "Do our control centers shift during the day, or are we controlled exclusively by one center?" "Do our control centers change as we grow older?" Inform students that the centers do change—and they change often—during any given day depending on the circumstances. I feel that control centers change somewhat as we grow older, and I also believe that we can classify ourselves to some extent with one dominant center. The important element here is that the body-center theory is an excellent way to create physicality for the role the actors are currently preparing.

Allow scene study partners to get together and discuss the control centers in relation to their characters. Tell them to experiment with movement for their characters.

Objectives:

The student will:

- learn what factors in our lives create body language
- learn the four major body control centers and their relation to body language and movement
- explore how control centers affect them
- determine body control centers for the characters in the scenes being studied

Lessons 24–25
Comedy Scene Study

Commentary
See the commentary for Lessons 13–14.

Lesson 24
The Comedy Scene Assignment

Materials:
Pre-selected Comedy Scenes
Script Analysis Sheets
Scenework Progress Charts
(All may be found in Part III, Scene Study)

Procedure:
Having just completed the performance of the psychophysical scene, students are anxious to begin a new scene, one which is different (comedy) and one which teams them up with a new partner.

I would like to caution teachers that these scenes, like the psychophysical scenes, must be carefully chosen for each actor. The goal is to correct major acting problems, stretch the actor, and help him develop his craft. It often takes me weeks to select just the right scene, and to team up each actor with just the right partner. This process obviously calls for the utmost care and sensitivity from the teacher.

Tell students that you will give them their new comedy scenes today. Comedy techniques will be dealt with in future classes. Today they will become acquainted with the scenes. Ask students to meet with their scene-study partners in a comfortable and private part of the theater to read the scenes aloud. Explain that you will travel to each group to see if there are any questions or concerns.

Remind students that the Scenework Progress Chart must be filled out for every rehearsal. You are also giving them a copy of the Script Analysis Sheet so that they may begin to think about the answers to those questions also.

Objectives:
The student will:
- be made aware of expectations of the comedy scene study unit
- become familiar with the pre-selected comedy scene and partner

Lesson 25

Performing the Comedy Scene

Several classes will now be devoted to the performance of the comedy scenes currently being worked on. The teacher is, by now, familiar with the procedure of scene presentation and post-scene critique, but refer to the Scene Study Unit if there are any questions.

Materials:
actors in the scene being presented will bring in their own props, costumes, etc.
Scene Evaluation Form
video recorder, tape, tripod

Procedure
As the actors prepare to perform, give the class the necessary information (name of scene, playwright, actors' and characters' names, etc.).

Tell the class to take brief notes on the back of the evaluation sheet during the scene. Students do not want to take so many notes that they miss a substantial part of the performance.

The scene is performed and videotaped.

At the completion of the scene, the actors discuss the Script Analysis Sheet, telling what the scene is about ("This is the story of what happens when . . ."), the characters' objectives, and the climax.

The next step is the post-performance critique (see Part III, Scene Study).

The instructor works with the actors to correct major acting problems in the scene.

The Scene Evaluation Forms are completed by the class as homework, handed in the next class, and given to the actors as feedback from colleagues.

Objectives:
The student will:
- perform a comedy scene from a play (with costumes, props, set)
- critique the scene according to proper procedure
- complete the Scene Evaluation Form
- analyze the scene from a literary/performance point of view
- correct acting problems through teacher coaching
- apply lesson to his own acting problems

Lessons 26–30
The Techniques of Comedy Acting

Commentary

Comedy is very popular and a lot of fun—but also difficult to teach. Much of it is based on timing: when to deliver that line, when to make that gesture or that grimace, when to take that pratfall. There are many teachers who feel that timing is inborn and cannot be taught. This is a defeatist attitude! While I feel there certainly are comic geniuses with impeccable timing, all actors can be taught an appreciation for comedy and how to bring a playwright's comic script to life. Energy and enthusiasm are what's needed in this unit.

The following lessons should be a source of great enjoyment. People all over the world laugh, and usually they laugh at the same things: others falling, walking into walls, getting trapped in revolving doors (as long as the victim does not get hurt), the arrogant teacher who delivers a lecture with the zipper of his trousers open (yes, a true story), animals with human characteristics, humans with animal characteristics, the story of the fish that got away, etc. Comedy was a major form of entertainment as far back as the Greeks, and comic "stock characters" were enormously popular in the commedia dell'arte. Our comic tradition, then, has a rich heritage several thousand years old.

Lessons 26 and 27 concern four comedy techniques: topping, expectation and surprise, embarrassment, and farce. John Louis Dezseran was instrumental in inspiring these, and his *Student Actor's Handbook* offers an excellent chapter on comedy. Lessons 28 and 29, involving much class activity, have been taught through gales of laughter! Lesson 30 provides a more complete list of comic elements, followed by the showing of a video or movie of some of the comedy masters wherein those elements may be identified. I feel that the movie is important so that student actors can actually witness the techniques at work by such notables as Laurel and Hardy, Lucille Ball, Charlie Chaplin, Abbott and Costello, etc. The students should then be able to identify the techniques in their current scene-study unit.

A general note: Comedy requires a spirit of fun. Try to infuse these lessons with joy rather than getting too analytical. At least in dramatic terms, the "serious" study of comedy is inherently ludicrous.

Lesson 26

"Topping" and "Embarrassment"

Materials:
some furniture pieces for improvisational use

Procedure:
This lesson will serve as an introduction to comedy.

Part I:
Set up the following improvisation.

Improvisation 1: Four or five girls are sitting in their college dormitory room discussing last night's dates. Girl A relates her story. Then Girl B must "top" Girl A's story, or make her story more exciting than the previous one. Girl C tops Girl B's story, and so on until all five have had a chance. Girl E's story will probably be outrageous, and so it should be!

Ask the class to determine why this improvisation is funny. What technique would you say this improvisation demonstrates? You may simply call the technique "topping".

You, the teacher, should tell the improv performers the plot of the improv privately, that is, do not let the class hear it before seeing the improv. You need the sense of surprise and spontaneity for the improv to properly work.

After the discussion about the improv, tell the students that today we will explore comedy. Begin with the question, *"What makes people laugh?"* This question can spark a very interesting as well as amusing discussion. Ask students to give examples of funny moments. Answers may range from "embarrassing moments" to outright slapstick.

Part II:
Set up the following improvisation. Again, tell the plot to the performers privately.

Improvisation 2: Two people, a man and a woman, are on a cruise ship in the South Pacific. The man is looking for an empty deck chair and finds one next to the woman, who is enjoying the sun. They begin a conversation, trying to impress each other. Thus far, this improv is similar to Improv 1. However, at one point, a third character enters and must destroy the credibility of one of the two people. ("John, why are you sitting here? You haven't cleaned the latrines on the lower deck!")

The comedy occurs due to embarrassment or discrediting the character. Have the class provide examples of times when they have been embarrassed or witnessed others embarrassed.

Objectives:
The student will:
- explore reasons for laughter
- identify two basic comedy techniques
- use the body and voice to create comedy

Lesson 27

"Expectation and Surprise" and "Farce"

Materials:
some furniture for improvisational use

Procedure:
This lesson is Part 2 of the comedy unit

Part I:
Review the comedy techniques learned during the previous class. Ask the students if they have seen anything that would exemplify those techniques since that class.

Part II:
We will now do two more improvisations that illustrate a basic comedy technique.

Improvisation 3: Three professors in a laboratory are about to make a major scientific breakthrough. As they discuss the benefits of their discovery for all of mankind, one of the scientists gradually takes on the characteristics—physically and vocally—of a caveman. The others do not react to the change. Rather, they continue their work. Soon another begins the process, and then the third. The improv ends when all three are totally transformed, with the accompanying lumbering movements and grunts and growls!

This technique is called "expectation and surprise." We are led to believe one thing, and we are surprised by a totally different outcome. We see this in the circus when a strongman cannot lift what appears to be a barbell of enormous weight. When he gives up, a clown or a child comes along and easily lifts it and carries it off.

Ask the class to identify some of their favorite comedy actors. Discuss why these actors are funny. You should elicit answers that include the use of the body and voice. Explain how actors need to be so versatile in the use of these two tools.

Improvisation 4: A is attempting to sell a "magic hen" to B (have an actor play the hen also). A must convince B of the hen's ability grant any wish. B buys the hen, and brings it home. B's spouse makes such a commotion about how B was cheated that B makes a wish that the spouse would turn into a turkey just to be quiet. The magic works! The spouse is transformed! The turkey now is attracted to the magic hen, and the two of them go off together!

This last of the four major techniques is "farce." The entire situation is unbelievable from the start (in "expectation and surprise," the situation is at first realistic).

Objectives:

The student will:
- identify the last two of the major comedy techniques
- use the body and voice to create comedy
- identify comedic situations in everyday life

Lesson 28
Using Voice and Body in Comedy Acting

Materials:
some furniture for improvisational use

Procedure:

Part I:
Review the four major comedy techniques.

Talk about the use of voice and body in comedy, using examples from student-performed improvs over the last two classes. Today we will explore further use of the body and voice in comedy.

Ask for two volunteers to perform an improv. Again, the "givens" are related to them privately. They are to perform the following situation:

Improvisation 1: A woman comes home from work and begins to read the mail. One letter is from her landlord, telling her that the rent is to be increased. She is very angry and calls the landlord to complain. Her husband enters and she relates the news to him. He is also angry and calls the landlord to express his displeasure. Finally, the landlord arrives to explain why he is raising the rent. The husband does not agree with the reasoning and pulls out two swords. He and the landlord duel and both kill each other. The woman finds money in the pockets of both the husband and the landlord and runs off happily.

During this improv, the actors may use only one word each. They may repeat the word, or parts of the word as many times as they would like, but they can use only that word. Select words with many or interesting syllables in it. For example, "gollywopper," "anticipatory," "liverwurst." The actor may choose to use the whole word or any part, such as "liverwurst" or "wurst" or "ver," etc.

Ask the class how communication occurs in an improv such as this, where there is no intelligible language. They will discuss body language, movement, gesture, and sound.

Improvisation 2: Two girls are excitedly discussing new engagements when they realize they are both engaged to the same man!

They become very angry and call him up to come to the house immediately and explain himself. He enters and is really on the spot. He tries to explain, but the girls get so upset that the mother of one enters to find out what the disturbance is about. She calms them all down but is infatuated with the young man, and he with her! The improv ends with the mother and the young man exiting together, ready to elope.

Again, select one word for each actor to use.

Part II:

We will now discuss comedy voices.

There are four basic comedy voices. The teacher should demonstrate the voices or ask students to try them:

HIGH NASAL: a nasal voice in a high pitch

LOW NASAL: a nasal voice in a low pitch

DUMB VOICE: a deeper-pitch, hollow voice

MECHANICAL: a voice which shows no variation in vocal quality (pitch, volume, etc.). This kind of voice is usually found in characters who must work impersonally and quickly (e.g., fast-food salespeople)

Have the students attempt all four types of comedy voices and give some examples of the kind of character they would associate with the voices.

Objectives:

The student will:

- use the body and voice to create comedy
- learn the four basic comedy voices
- discuss types of comedic characters associated with comedy voices

Lesson 29

Creating Comedy from Environment and Circumstances

This is a fun lesson for the comedy unit.

Materials:
paper, pen (for teacher)
possibly some pieces of furniture or props

Procedure:
Tell the class that today's class will be improvisational in nature, and will also test their creativity and originality.

Ask the class to suggest some interesting environments. You should write these down on a piece of paper. My class came up with: a ski lift, a deserted island, a hot air balloon, the top of a ferris wheel, an attic, the rooftop of a New York City apartment building, the set of a TV show, to name a few!

Ask for two volunteers, and take them to a part of the space which will enable you to talk privately with them.

Ask them to quickly determine their relationship (husband-wife, brother-sister, teacher-student, friends, etc.).

Give them one of the environments from the list prepared by the class.

They must quickly come up with a brief plot in which there is one of the following progressions (assign the progression; do not give a choice):

1. Both actors begin at a "normal" tempo, and gradually make a transition into slow motion in movement and speech.

2. Both characters transform into animals.

3. Both characters begin speaking but shift into singing the entire piece (an opera).

4. Both characters begin in the Stone Age but end up in the future.

5. One character, a female, becomes a male, and the partner, a male, becomes a female.

6. An ugly person becomes beautiful and a beautiful person becomes ugly.

7. Both characters become sad after beginning elated.

8. Both characters become heavier and heavier until they cannot move or speak.

9. An ignorant person becomes a genius, and a genius becomes ignorant.

After the first improvisation, ask the class what changes occurred. Although this is an exaggerated comedy situation, what do we learn from it that can be applied to all acting? You should elicit the response that characters change during the course of a scene or play.

Note the use of voice and body in these improvisations. Comedy often calls upon the actor to exaggerate or use complex movement. Also, the voice must be versatile.

Proceed to the other improvisations.

Objectives:
The student will:
- note the physical and vocal versatility needed for comedy acting
- note the progression that occurs during a scene in terms of character change

Lesson 30
Achieving Comedy Onstage

Materials:
none

Procedure:
This lesson continues our study of comedy

Part I:
Tell students that today's lesson will deal with methods of achieving comedy onstage. They may want to determine which of these is used in the comedy scenes they are currently working on.

Review the four major comedy techniques learned thus far.

Part II:
Now we will learn additional ways to achieve comedy onstage:

1. *Intricate movement*
Movement in comedy is more intricate than in drama. Examples are slapstick and simultaneous movement. Observing some of the comedy "greats" (Laurel and Hardy, Lucille Ball, Charlie Chaplin, etc.) can attest to this.

2. *Exaggeration of the silhouette*
The actor should have an underlying view of how the character occupies space. Also, certain parts of the body may "lead" the actor. For example, follow the nose or the stomach or the hips. Ask students to try this.

3. *Establishing a character heavier or dumber than the actor*

4. *Establishing energy levels for various tasks.*
Audiences laugh at either too little or too much energy—for example, picking up a book that one supposes to be very light, but is in fact extremely heavy. This is evidenced in the circus when the strongman attempts to pick up the "heavy" barbells but cannot. Then a clown or child comes along, picks up the barbells, and walks off.

The difference between what the audience expects and what it gets causes the laugh.

5. *Repertoire of tones*
There are various comedy voices:

DEAD VOICE: this voice has absolutely no enthusiasm

EXAGGERATION OF A TYPE: a language associated with a certain "type" of person (e.g., a gangster, a professor, etc.) and then exaggerated

NASAL VOICES: there are two kinds, low nasal and high nasal

DUMB VOICE

6. *A variety of accents and dialects*

7. *Changes in the face, body, and voice*
There are dozens of changes and things to do with these three (squeaks, growls, blank faces, "prune" face, short body, tall, thin, loose-jointed, etc.). Again, you may want students to experiment with these.

8. *Overdramatizing*

9. *De-personalizing*
This involves taking the human element out of the work and making it mechanical.

10. *Exaggeration of a style*
This deals with a period of history or style of acting.

11. *Knowing the value of costumes and disguise*
Try different adjustments with a hat to illustrate this. Try the rim down, up; wear it askew. The mood changes with each.

12. *Timing*
This element is extremely important in comedy! Movement and speaking must be timed, that is, there should be varying rates of speed to suit the moment.

13. *Teamwork*
Another important aspect of comedy! Often an actor will need to mute a line so the other actor will get the laugh. It is important to play *with* your partner in comedy.

14. *Mastering many speeds*

15. *Energy!*
Energy is the most important element in comedy.

Objectives:
The student will:
- review the four major comedy techniques
- learn new methods of creating comedy onstage
- experiment with voice, body, and face to illustrate new comedy techniques

Extension:

Show the class a comedy classic featuring such masters as Laurel and Hardy, Lucille Ball, Charlie Chaplin, the Marx Brothers, Abbott and Costello, etc. These films are available at the library or local video stores. Ask the class to give examples of the various comedy techniques illustrated. It is valuable for the student actors to see the masters at work. This will provide fun, and the students will be able to see the practical application of the exercises they have done.

Lessons 31–40
Voice and Speech

Commentary

Voice and speech study is obviously important in the training of an actor. As voice and body are the tools the actor uses to create every character, theater teachers are obligated to begin this study as early as possible.

The extent of work in this area will reflect the teacher's personal training, but expectations to some degree should be included for the following areas:

• the breathing process

• proper diaphragmatic control in breathing for the stage

• the phonation process

• flexibility of the voice

• the various elements of voice and speech, including resonance, pitch, tempo, volume, diction, emphasis, phrasing, interpretation,

• proper diction

• correction of major voice and speech problems

• a relaxed throat

An assignment of some kind—whether it is a reading as in Lesson 34, or special attention to voice and speech in scene study—should accompany this unit, for the practical application of classroom theory is necessary. A Theater Voice and Speech Rating Sheet is provided in Lesson 34 as an evaluative tool, and also to provide feedback for the student.

Teachers are advised to examine this unit closely prior to teaching it. Some of the materials needed must be prepared in advance, such as the vocal tape, which contains examples of the best of stage speech. In addition, a knowledge of the phonetic alphabet is helpful, but not absolutely necessary, in teaching this unit.

You may apply this work to specific classes, using the suggested plans in a manner that best suits your purposes.

These lessons are sequential, progressing from stage breathing to phonation (producing sound) to articulation (the "cutting" of the sound into intelligible units for communication). The last area of study is resonation.

More specifically, Lessons 31 and 32 introduce the idea of breathing for the stage, which is different from breathing to stay alive. There are many exercises for training an actor to breathe properly. Use the books listed in the bibliography for additional work in this area. Evangeline Machlin's book *Speech for the Stage* is particularly effective. I took a workshop with her once and can only sing this wonderful teacher's praises.

Lesson 33 is about the production of sound, or phonation, and includes a diagram of vocal anatomy. Lessons 34 and 35 deal with a "reading" as a performance assignment. Here attention is paid to proper breathing, phonation, and articulation. Lessons 36 and 37 and the accompanying Articulation Worksheets provide practice for that reading. The use of the rating sheet in Lessons 34 and 35 should be explained carefully to the class, and each of the eleven categories should be meticulously defined by the teacher. Leave approximately a week between assigning the reading and the performance, during which you may go on to other voice and articulation lessons. During the performance of the reading, the class should listen to the entire piece before circling the appropriate evaluation in each category. The actor should repeat the reading a second and possibly a third time so the class has the opportunity of observing all necessary areas.

Lessons 38 and 39 are concerned with resonance, or depth and richness of sound. If you choose to teach the phonetic symbols in Lesson 39 and discuss Standard Stage Speech, it is advisable to inform the students that this provides a "norm" from which the actor departs depending upon the character and the various elements that would comprise his speech (e.g., section of the country, level of education, etc.). After all, an actor wants an *appropriate* sound, which depends on the character. Stanley and Blanche, of *A Streetcar Named Desire,* do not possess the "fine" and "pleasant" sounds these lessons try to evoke. We should always keep in mind that these lessons must serve the actor's purpose, and that Standard Stage Speech allows for flexibility rather than uniformity through the imposition of a specific sound.

Lesson 40 calls for a prepared tape of excellent examples of stage speech. This needs to be prepared in advance. Again, libraries are a good source of recordings of classics performed by well-trained actors.

Lesson 31

The Breathing Process

Materials:
none

Procedure:
Today's lesson begins a series of instructional plans dealing with theater voice and diction.

Part I:
Tell students that it is necessary to study theater voice and diction because an actor has only two tools—his body and his voice. Each must be extremely flexible and be able to create an endless line of characters, and the voice must be trained to communicate meaning and emotion.

With this discussion underway, ask what the difference is between voice and speech (the former is concerned with being heard, and the latter is concerned with being understood).

Part II:
We will now deal with parts of the voice and speech mechanism.

Breathing is an integral part of voice production. It is the first step in producing sound or speech.

Break down the breathing process into its components: inhalation and exhalation.

Inhalation: The muscle known as the diaphragm (locate it for students as you demonstrate before the class) lowers. This lowering increases the amount of room for the expansion of the lungs. Air is sucked into the body through the nose or mouth and travels quickly to the rear of the mouth, down the bronchial tubes and into the lungs.

Exhalation: The diaphragm relaxes, returning to its original position. This squeezes the air out of the lungs, up the trachea, into the mouth, and out of the body.

Students may be aware of the term *diaphragmatic breathing.* Acting teachers and singing teachers use it all the time. Actually, everyone already breathes diaphragmatically. We have no choice! However, control of the diaphragm in breathing enables us to better regulate both the intake and outflow of air. This will add quality to the voice, enable us to speak long passages, and also enable us to be heard in the rear of the theater. Proper breathing is a necessity for the well-trained actor.

Part III:

It is now time for the students to experiment with diaphragmatic breathing. Ask them to stand up and spread themselves throughout the space.

It is a good idea to start with warm-up exercises as students begin their breathing work. This will not only relax them but begin the process of associating exercising with all voice work. Have students do basic shake-outs, neck rolls, etc.

Ask the students to lie down. They should align the body so that the small of the back is in a straight line with the back of the neck. Students should put a hand on the stomach and feel it rise and fall with each breath. Explain that diaphragmatic breathing is very noticeable in this position because the rib cage is forced up and out by the floor. "Chest breathing" is very nearly impossible in this position.

Another way to introduce this is to have a volunteer lie down and have the class gather round. Place an object of some weight (a small book, a wallet, etc.) on the student's stomach. Diaphragmatic breathing is now plainly visible as the object rises and falls. Students may place similar objects on their own stomachs as they explore this exercise.

One more exercise will increase awareness of the diaphragm:

Students are still on the floor, aligned and on their backs. Explain the exercise before students attempt it. Students will inhale *into the chest*. With the chest expanded, they will then *send the air down into the stomach*. If students place one hand on the chest and one on the stomach, it will be easy for them to feel the movement in the respective hands (i.e., the "chest hand" will elevate with the initial inhalation; it will then lower when the air is sent to the stomach, and the "stomach hand" will elevate, etc.). The third step is to take the same air, which is now in the stomach, and *send it up into the chest once again*. The fourth step is to blow the air out hard through the mouth.

This exercise allows students to feel the different places where air is directed. However, it is a difficult exercise, and the teacher should use judgment as to whether this particular class is "ready" for it.

The number of repetitions of the exercise should never exceed five. Leave 20 seconds between repetitions.

As your class time will nearly be over, instruct students to roll to one side and sit up slowly. Then they may stand. Caution students never to move suddenly and quickly after breathing exercises, for this may cause temporary light-headedness. Allay any fears, however, and tell them that if this should occur, the student should sit down and lower his head for a moment. Such episodes are *not* dangerous.

Objectives:
The student will:
- learn the importance of proper breathing in voice/sound production
- learn the necessity of diaphragmatic control
- practice diaphragmatic control
- distinguish between voice and speech
- learn the importance of a properly trained voice

Lesson 32
Using the Diaphragm

Materials:
lengths of rope approximately 40″ to 45″ long; one rope per student

Procedure:
Today's lesson will continue to explore diaphragmatic breathing.

Review the major points of yesterday's lesson, stressing the importance of proper stage breathing. Today we will continue to do exercises to help us control the diaphragm, as well as reinforce the sensation of diaphragmatic rather than chest breathing.

Students should spread out in the space, making sure they feel free and unencumbered by others close to them. They should also be encouraged to take off shoes, sweaters, or anything else that may prevent a feeling of relaxation. Begin with basic warm-ups. Of special importance is a properly executed spine fold. Students should be aware that the vertebrae must stack one on top of the other as they rise; the neck and the head are last, and each is treated separately. Often students will bring both up as one body part, creating tension in the neck and shoulder muscles.

The instructor should talk about the similarity between the spine fold and aligning oneself on the floor. A properly aligned body reduces muscular tension.

Give each student a length of rope. Students should place the rope around the body, chest high, with the rope passing under the armpits. Pull the rope snugly, and cross one end over the other in front of the body. Chest breathing is made obvious as the pressure of the rope is felt. The point where the two ends of the rope cross will change on the inhale because the chest expansion will use more of the rope's length. Students should then lower the rope until it is over the diaphragm. Repeat the process. This exercise is a graphic illustration of body expansion during breathing. The rope should be lowered to the waist also to show how air fills the lower back and sides during diaphragmatic breathing. *All of this air is usable.* Imagine the potential when an actor can tap into this air supply!

The next exercise is the "Football Crouch." Have students assume a position like football players "on the line." One arm supports the body, which is now in a crouched position. Tell students to place the free hand on the stomach. This position is another which shows proper breathing, for the breathing is forced to be diaphragmatic.

Students should then lie on the floor. Place a small, weighted object on the diaphragm. (This exercise may have been done during yesterday's lesson. It should be done again.) Tell students to feel the object as it rises and then lowers in accordance with proper breathing.

Now have students try to force the object as high as it will comfortably go during an inhalation. Try this a few times.

With the object in a raised position, have students exhale, projecting the tone "Ah." Tell them the mouth should be opened wide, and the object should return to its starting position in a smooth, unjerky manner. This teaches smooth exhalation and begins to instruct students how to control exhalation.

The projected tone can be tried a few times until students feel comfortable with it.

Have students stand (slowly) and try the projected tone with one hand on the stomach and one hand on the chest. The "chest hand" should not move. If there is difficulty with this, the student may again do it lying down. Explain that the problem many students have breathing with diaphragmatic control from a standing position is often due to gravity and its pull on the rib cage. During proper breathing, the rib cage is up and out. If anyone is encountering difficulty, make sure he knows that retraining his breathing process is no easy task but will come with time and exercise.

Objectives:
The student will:
  • practice proper diaphragmatic control during breathing

Lesson 33

Phonation

Materials:
Vocal Anatomy diagram (following this lesson)
mirrors if available

Procedure:
This is the third lesson in the voice and speech unit. Today we will review breathing and begin phonation.

Part I:
Ask for student volunteers to discuss

Inhalation: Air drawn into mouth or nose to back of throat (pharynx) and down trachea (windpipe) to bronchi to lungs. Simultaneously, the diaphragm lowers and the ribs are pulled upward and out by the intercostal muscles (between the ribs) to allow more space for lung expansion.

Exhalation: Diaphragm relaxes to initial position and ribs lower. Air is forced by these movements out of the lungs, up the trachea, into the mouth and out (via mouth or nose).

Part II:
Now we will discuss *phonation.* Ask the class if anyone knows what phonation means. It means "The act or process of producing speech sounds." Therefore, we will now explore how sound is produced.

Use the accompanying Vocal Anatomy diagram.

As air is forced up the trachea, it must pass through the top of the trachea, called the *larynx.* At the top of the larynx are the vocal cords. Refer to the inset picture on the diagram. Notice how the cords form a "V" when the actor is not speaking. Air passes through them easily. The space between the cords is called the *glottis.*

During phonation, or when making sound, the cords snap together. The air traveling up the trachea passes over the closed cords, creating vibrations. These vibrations travel into the *resonating cavities,* where they produce sound. The resonating cavities are the throat, the nose, and the mouth.

Actors must work for the proper distribution of sound in the three resonating cavities. Too many sound vibrations held in the throat will cause a "tight" sound; sometimes it can sound "gravelly."

(This is called "glottal friction" and is caused by too little air over the vocal cords, with resonation mainly in the throat.) If too much air is resonated mainly in the mouth, a "hollow" effect may occur, and if too much air is directed to the nasal resonating cavity, a nasal effect (good for comedy) will occur.

Nasal resonance should occur only on the sounds *m, n, ng.*

Have students touch the sides of their noses to feel the vibrations on these three sounds. Try saying the word *hungry*. Make sure students say it very slowly. There should be no nasal vibrations on the *hu-*. Students should feel vibrations on the nose on *-ng-*; the vibrations stop on *-ry*.

The *uvula* is found at the back of the soft palate. It serves to open or close the passageway to the nose for air to travel through. Using *hungry* again, students, if they say the word slowly enough, will actually *feel* the uvula snap closed on *-ry* so that no further air is allowed in the nose. Words such as *hungry, angry, anger,* etc., can help strengthen control of the uvula if practiced often.

If the instructor has access to mirrors, students can practice *hungry,* watching themselves in the mirror. They will be able to actually see the uvula rise and lower. It is good idea to have mirrors on hand for voice work so students can see lip shapes, vowel shapes, etc.

Objectives:
The student will:
- review breathing procedure
- define phonation
- learn the definitions of larynx, vocal cords, glottis, resonance, uvula
- identify the three resonating cavities
- learn how nasal resonance is produced

VOCAL ANATOMY

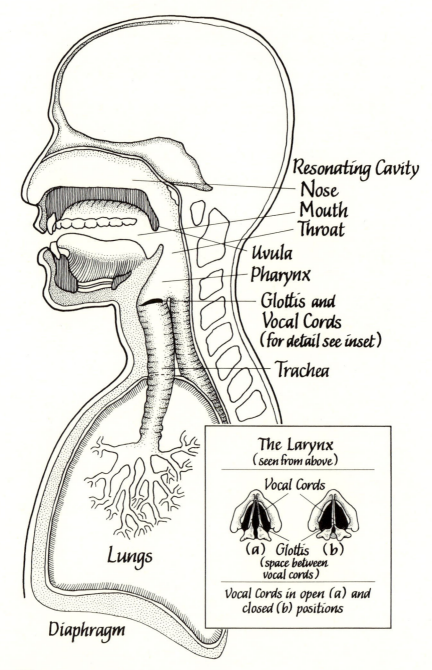

Resonating Cavity
Nose
Mouth
Throat

Uvula

Pharynx

Glottis and
Vocal Cords
(for detail see inset)

Trachea

Lungs

Diaphragm

The Larynx
(seen from above)

Vocal Cords

(a) Glottis (b)
(space between
vocal cords)

Vocal Cords in open (a) and
closed (b) positions

Lesson 34

The Elements of Voice and Speech

Materials:
Theater Voice and Speech Rating Sheet (following this lesson)

Procedure:
Tell the class that thus far in our voice and speech unit we have dealt with breathing and phonation. Today we will deal with the elements of voice and speech.

Distribute the Theater Voice and Speech Rating Sheet. Inform students that this sheet is an evaluative tool in responding to someone's voice and speech.

The eleven areas noted on the sheet are important for proper voice and speech production. Discuss the sheet with the class and entertain questions. The Vocal Anatomy diagram, used in Lesson 33, may be helpful as you discuss this work (especially for dealing with resonance and phonation). *It is important that students understand each of the eleven elements.*

Assignment: Prepare a one-two minute reading.
This reading does not have to be memorized but should be familiar enough that the reader needs merely to glance at it every so often. It should also be of interest to the reader. All too often the actor selects material which lacks imagery and opportunity. These readings are instructional tools, but should be interesting to the listeners. The reading may be a poem, part of a short story or essay, lyrics of a song, etc. Students should pencil in a slash mark to denote places for inhalation. These marks can then be adjusted when working with the student to improve this area of performance.

As noted, the Theater Voice and Speech Rating Sheet is a tool to evaluate the readings. Performers are given a rating sheet by each member of the class. When filling out the sheet:

1. Circle the appropriate evaluation in each category.

2. Circle the appropriate overall impression. The numbers run from 1, or work that is ineffective, to 5, or superb work.

3. Write some comments for the actor. These provide valuable feedback after the actor has put considerable preparation into the performance.

Objectives:

The student will:

- learn the various elements of voice and speech production, including:

posture	pitch
breathing	emphasis
phrasing	tempo
phonation	resonance
volume	interpretation
diction	

- learn how to complete the rating sheet
- prepare a one-minute reading, with careful attention paid to voice and speech elements, to present to the class
- critique others' voice and speech using the rating sheet
- improve listening skills

Theater Voice and Speech Rating Sheet

Actor's Name _____

Reviewer's Name _____

Circle your evaluation of the actor's work in each of the following categories. This review sheet also includes space for comments.

1. **Posture**
   proper posture; body is aligned; vertebrae stacked one on top of the other | Off-balanced; uncentered | too stiff

2. **Breathing**
   firm breath support; proper diaphragmatic breathing | shallow breathing; diaphragm not working to capacity | chest breathing

3. **Phrasing**
   effective choice of breath groups | intervals are too brief between breaths; lack of cohesiveness in idea/ image creation | Intervals are too long; actor is running out of air

4. **Phonation** (Sound)
   (a) phonation is full-bodied; there is depth to the voice; excellent nuances of sound | too breathy | too harsh

   (b) throat is relaxed; initial sounds are comfortable and smooth | glottal friction; too little air over vocal cords | attack is too hard

5. **Volume**
   (a) comfortable volume | too soft | too loud

   (b) beginning sounds audible | beginning sounds inaudible | beginning sounds harsh

   (c) ending sounds audible | ending sounds inaudible | ending sounds harsh

6. **Diction**
   proper diction; sounds are shaped through proper use of tongue, lips, teeth | slurred speech | over-articulation

(continued on next page)

7. **Pitch**
   comfortable pitch; meaning controls pitch variety | pitch is too high | pitch is too low

8. **Emphasis**
   interesting emphasis through carefully selected variety of volume, pitch, duration, tempo | monotone delivery; not enough emphasis to distinguish important elements | artificial melody; too much emphasis (sing-song delivery)

9. **Tempo**
   comfortable rate of delivery | too slow | too fast

10. **Resonance**
    (a) effective use of nasal cavity | de-nasal | nasal

    (b) effective use of oral resonator | hollow | thin

    (c) effective use of pharyngeal resonator | breathy | tense; strident

11. **Meaning/Interpretation**
    sounds and meaning merge for effective communication | lack of connection with meaning; artificial delivery | lack of connection with meaning; artificial delivery

Overall Impression

Did this oral delivery work for you?

1	2	3	4	5
No, it did not	Somewhat, but it could have been better	It was good; some elements worked well	It was effective; I found it well-prepared and interesting	Superb! Excellent attention to vocal elements and message communicated beautifully

Comments

Lesson 35
Readings for Voice and Speech

Materials:
readings brought in by students
Theater Voice and Speech Rating Sheets

Procedure:
Today we begin the presentation of readings assigned in Lesson 34.

Part I:
Do some basic warm-up exercises, concentrating specifically on vocals (spine fold, head roll, face massage, face tightening and expanding, tongue stretchers, diction exercises, etc.). Students should hum throughout to warm up the voice.

Obviously, the number of exercises will be determined by the length of the class and the number of presenters. I usually have two, sometimes three, presenters per class. A single presenter would have the opportunity of having much work done on his voice. Often, however, a single presenter is not practical, especially if the class is large.

Part II:
Hand out the Theater Voice and Speech Rating Sheets. Explain the procedure:

1. The reader will present. The class is not to take notes or deal with the rating sheet at all during the initial reading because it is only a minute long, and the class will miss it if the students are busy writing.

2. The reader will present a part of the reading again. The class may now circle the appropriate areas on the rating sheet, as well as take notes.

3. Feel free to ask the reader to repeat a section once again. It is difficult for the class to observe all eleven items on the rating sheet with one or two readings.

4. The instructor should work with the student to correct voice and speech problems. This is where the instructor's own expertise comes in. Even without a great deal of training, the teacher can isolate and correct simple problems. I feel it is important for the

student to correct at least one problem. The positive reinforcement is necessary for future progress.

Objectives:

The student will:
- warm up the voice
- present a reading
- critique a reading
- as a presenter, will correct one speech/voice problem
- practice listening skills

Lesson 36
The Components of Articulation

Materials:
Articulation Worksheet
tape recorder and tape

Procedure:

Part I:
The first part of today's lesson in theater voice and speech will deal with the components of articulation.

Identify for your students the moveable parts: the soft palate, the tongue, the lips, the jaw, and the cheeks (although this works with the jaw). Identify the immoveable parts: the teeth and the hard palate.

All of these parts work together to shape sound into communicable elements we call language.

These parts "cut," "shape," and "mold" sound. Speech problems are often linked to incorrect use of these parts, such as incorrect tongue placement or jaw movement, or mouths that do not open wide enough for vowel sounds.

It is important, then, that we learn to "work" those parts well in order to produce the best possible product: language that is clear and understandable and has a truly fine, pleasant sound.

Part II:
Students should sit comfortably in their chairs with their feet firmly on the floor and their hands resting on the thighs.

A few exercises should now be done to relax the throat for the articulation work to follow. The students should hum through as much of this as possible to warm up the vocal cords.

The exercises should include:

1. slow, gentle head rolls
2. head turns (medium speed): right–center–left–center, right–center–left–center, etc.
3. tightening the face and expanding it (this warms up facial muscles)
4. pursing the lips very tight and relax
5. yawning (yawns relax the throat. These can be induced by opening the mouth very wide while inhaling to the back of the

throat; at the same time, tilt the head back and begin a falsetto sound, lowering the sound and the head simultaneously. This takes time to learn but can prove beneficial. Also, yawns are contagious, and as soon as one student yawns, the others will follow).

Part III:

Students should stand. Give them the Articulation Worksheets.

These worksheets contain full and partial poems. You may want to explain to the students that poetry is often the best material to use when studying voice and speech because the sounds that comprise the words are carefully selected by the poets. They certainly are beautiful, and this elevated language provides ample opportunity to study and learn. The fact that these examples are *not* written in ordinary discursive prose should and will draw fully on the actor's vocal resources, while challenging both the intellect and the imagination.

Work with these sheets as you deem best. You may want students to read only two lines each, or you may want the class to read them in unison. Often the latter is the best method to begin with as students will not feel "on the spot" immediately.

Listen carefully as each student reads, and help that individual with diction and "playing the sound." I like to use a high-quality tape recorder and allow students to hear and assess their voices. Point out areas that are good, and also point out areas that need attention. Correct diction problems and tempo. I find that one of the biggest problems is the speed with which actors read. Make them slow down so we can hear the sounds!

Make sure each person has a chance to read. Students should also demonstrate diaphragmatic control as they read.

Needless to say, bad speaking habits are not easy to mend. This lesson is one of the first steps. Impress upon the students that *listening* is extremely important in voice work. Listening is the "feedback" system. They need to sensitize the ear in order to correct the sound.

Objectives:

The student will:
- learn the components of articulation
- warm up the voice and relax the throat through exercises
- read passages from the Voice and Speech Articulation worksheets and correct articulation problems
- learn the importance of a well-trained ear in voice and speech work

Articulation Worksheet

Passages for practice

1. When the green woods laugh with the voice of joy,
   And the dimpling stream runs laughing by;
   When the air does laugh with our merry wit,
   And the green hill laughs with the noise of it;
   When the meadows laugh with lively green,
   And the grasshopper laughs in the merry scene,
   When Mary and Susan and Emily
   With their sweet round mouths sing "Ha, Ha, He!"
   When the painted birds laugh in the shade,
   Where our table with cherries and nuts is spread,
   Come live and be merry, and join with me,
   To sing the sweet chorus of "Ha, Ha, He!"
   —William Blake, "Nurse's Song"

2. Tyger! Tyger! burning bright
   In the forests of the night,
   What immortal hand or eye
   Could frame thy fearful symmetry?
   —William Blake, "The Tyger"

3. The sun descending in the west,
   The evening star does shine;
   The birds are silent in their nest,
   And I must seek for mine.
   The moon like a flower
   In heaven's high bower,
   With silent delight
   Sits and smiles on the night.
   —William Blake, "Night"

4. She walks in beauty, like the night
   Of cloudless climes and starry skies;
   And all that's best of dark and bright
   Meet in her aspect and her eyes:
   Thus mellow'd to that tender light
   Which heaven to gaudy day denies.

And on that cheek, and o'er that brow,
So soft, so calm, yet eloquent,
The smiles that win, the tints that glow,
But tell of days in goodness spent,
A mind at peace with all below,
A heart whose love is innocent!
      —Lord Byron, "She Walks in Beauty"

5. And a youth said, Speak to us of Friendship.
And he answered, saying:
Your friend is your needs answered.
And when he is silent your heart ceases
not to listen to his heart;
For without words, in friendship, all thought,
all desires, all expectations are born
and shared, with joy that is unacclaimed.
When you part from your friend, you grieve not;
For that which you love most in him may be
clearer in his absence, as the mountain
to the climber is clearer from the plain.
      —Kahlil Gibran, *The Prophet*

6. O, she doth teach the torches to burn bright!
It seems she hangs upon the cheek of night
Like a rich jewel in an Ethiop's ear;
Beauty too rich for use, for earth too dear!
      —William Shakespeare, *Romeo and Juliet*

7. My bounty is as boundless as the sea,
My love as deep; the more I give to thee,
The more I have, for both are infinite!
      —William Shakespeare, *Romeo and Juliet*

8. Is this a dagger which I see before me,
The handle toward my hand? Come, let me clutch thee.
I have thee not, and yet I see thee still.
Art thou not, fatal vision, sensible
To feeling as to sight? or art thou but
A dagger of the mind, a false creation
Proceeding from the heat-obsessed brain?
      —William Shakespeare, *Macbeth*

9. That which hath made them drunk hath made me bold;
   What hath quench'd them, hath given me fire.
   —William Shakespeare, *Macbeth*

10. A fool, a fool! I met a fool i' the forest,
    A motley fool; a miserable world!
    As I do live by food, I met a fool.
    —William Shakespeare, *As You Like It*

Some Shakespearean insults

11. You old withered crabtree

12. You untutored churl!

13. You silly sanctimonious ape of form!

14. You gross lout; you mindless slave!

15. You vile thing; you petty scrap!

16. You cretin-faced loon!

17. You simpering whoremaster!

18. You unlettered small lettered soul!

19. You lascivious fat-kindred rascal!

20. You butcher's apprentice!

21. You clap-eared knave!

22. You fitchling, pilfering scoundrel!

23. You irksome brawling scalding pestilence!

24. You green sickness carrion!

25. You tallow face!

26. You painted maypole!

27. You ignorant long-tongued babbling gossip!

28. You wretched puling fool; you whining mammet!

29. You baggage; you disobedient wretch!

30. You common gamester to the camp!

31. Sweet are the uses of adversity,
    Which, like the toad, ugly and venomous,
    Wears yet a precious jewel in his head;
    And this our life, exempt from public haunt,
    Finds tongues in trees, books in the running brooks,
    Sermons in stones, and good in everything.
    —William Shakespeare, *As You Like It*

32. Whose woods these are I think I know.
    His house is in the village though;
    He will not see me stopping here
    To watch his woods fill up with snow.
    My little horse must think it queer
    To stop without a farmhouse near
    Between the woods and frozen lake
    The darkest evening of the year.
    He gives his harness bells a shake
    To ask if there is some mistake.
    The only other sound's the sweep
    Of easy wind and downy flake.
    The woods are lovely, dark and deep,
    But I have promises to keep,
    And miles to go before I sleep,
    And miles to go before I sleep.
    —Robert Frost, "Stopping by Woods
    on a Snowy Evening"

33. She left the web, she left the loom,
    She made three paces through the room,
    She saw the water lily bloom,
    She saw the helmet and the plume,
    She looked down to Camelot.
    —Alfred, Lord Tennyson, "The Lady of Shalott"

Lesson 37
Articulation Exercises

Materials:
Articulation Worksheet (following this lesson)

Procedure:
Today we will work on articulation.

Part I: *Warm-ups*

1. Students should stand throughout the space. Each should feel comfortable. Begin with a deep breath, letting it out slowly.

2. Spine fold (see "Relaxation/Warm-up Exercises" in the Scene Study Unit).

3. At the completion of the spine fold, take another deep breath. Go immediately into:

4. Head roll (slowly)

5. Head turns. During all of the above, students should be humming to warm up the voice.

6. Slow massage from the jaw joints following jaw lines to the chin; repeat.

7. Squeeze face into a "prune." Expand wide; repeat a few times.

8. Blow out the lips several times.

9. With the tip of the tongue behind the front of the lower teeth, thrust it forward, arching it. Make the sound "EEEE" before the stretch, and "AAHHH" during the stretch; repeat. This exercises the tongue.

10. Make the sounds "K", "G" (hard G), "Y" to feel the tongue moving to positions on the roof of the mouth which are successively closer to the front.

11. Steele Exercise (for lips and tongue)

P	P	P	P
PP	PP	PP	PP
PPP	PPP	PPP	PPP
PPPP	PPPP	PPPP	PPPP

Repeat the above with B, T, D, K, G (hard G). (This exercise comes from Edith Warman Skinner's book, *Speak with Distinction.*)

12. Resonance Exercises. Repeat "MMMM—AAHHH" several times with the mouth open wide; place the fingertips on the nose to feel the nasal resonance on the "M."

MAH	MAY	MEE	MO	MOO
NAH	NAY	NEE	NO	NOO
LAH	LAY	LEE	LO	LOO
VAH	VAY	VEE	VO	VOO
ZAH	ZAY	ZEE	ZO	ZOO

13. Mama's a Mean Mama (increase speed as you repeat)

14. Baby's a Bad Baby (increase speed as you repeat)

15. Papa's a Poor Papa (increase speed as you repeat)

16. "The tip of the tongue, the lips and the teeth" (repeat, increasing speed)

Continue with the articulation worksheets, which should be distributed to students.

Take the needed amount of time to work with students. The passages are carefully selected for sounds and meaning. They offer much opportunity for student progress in voice and speech.

Objectives:

The student will
- warm up the throat and voice
- practice articulation drills
- correct problems in articulation

Articulation Worksheet

Passages for Practice

Exercises for lip and tongue flexibility:

1. I bought a batch of baking-powder and baked a batch of biscuits. I brought a big basket of biscuits back to the bakery and baked a basket of big biscuits. Then I took the big basket of biscuits and the basket of big biscuits and mixed the big baskets with the basket of biscuits that was next to the big basket and put a bunch of biscuits from the baskets into a box. Then I took the box of mixed biscuits and a biscuit mixer and the biscuit basket and brought the basket of biscuits and the box of mixed biscuits and the biscuit mixer back to the bakery and opened up a can of sardines.

2. Theophilus Thistle, the successful thistle sifter, in sifting a sieve full of unsifted thistles, thrust three thousand thistles through the thick of his thumb. Now if Theophilus Thistle, the successful thistle sifter, in sifting a sieve full of unsifted thistles, thrust three thousand thistles through the thick of his thumb, see that thou in sifting a sieve full of unsifted thistles, thrust not three thousand thistles through the thick of thy thumb. Success to the successful thistle sifter.

3. Esau Wood sawed wood. Esau Wood would saw wood. All the wood Esau Wood saw Esau Wood would saw. In other words, all the wood Esau saw to saw, Esau sought to saw. Oh, the wood Wood would saw! And oh the wood-saw with which Wood would saw wood! But one day, Wood's wood saw would saw no wood, and thus the wood Wood sawed was not the wood Wood would saw if Wood's wood-saw would saw wood. Now, Wood would saw wood with a wood-saw that would saw would, so Esau sought a saw that would saw wood. One day, Esau saw a saw saw wood as no other would-saw would saw wood. In fact, of all the wood-saws Wood ever saw saw wood, Wood never saw a wood-saw that would saw wood as the wood-saw Wood saw saw wood would saw wood, and I never saw a wood-saw that would saw as the wood-saw Wood saw would saw until I saw Esau Wood saw wood with the wood-saw Wood saw saw wood. Now Wood saws wood with the wood-saw Wood saw saw wood.

4. I thought I heard the thump and thud of thirty thick-shod hoofs
   Like thirty thousand hailstones thundering on the roofs;
   I think the thing I thought I heard was Arthur doing sums,
   Thudding with his thick-soled boots and thumping with his
   thumbs.

5. Amidst the mists and coldest frosts
   With stoutest wrists and loudest boasts
   He thrusts his fists against the posts
   And still insists he sees the ghosts.

6. A tutor who tooted the flute
   Tried to tutor two tooters to toot;
   Said the two to the tutor, "Is it harder to toot, or
   To tutor two tooters to toot?"

7. What a to-do to die today
   At twenty or two to two;
   A thing distinctly hard to say
   Yet harder still to do.
   For we'll beat a tattoo
   At twenty to two
   A ratatatatatatatatato
   And the dragon will come
   When he hears the drum
   At twenty or two to two today
   At twenty or two to two.

8. To sit in solemn silence on a dull dark, dock,
   In a pestilential prison with a life-long lock;
   Awaiting the sensation of a short, sharp shock
   From a cheap and chipper chopper on a big blank block.
           —Gilbert and Sullivan, *The Mikado*

9. Gold, gold, gold, gold,
   Bright and yellow, hard and cold
   Molten, graven, hammered, rolled,
   Heavy to get and light to hold.
           —Thomas Hood, "Miss Kilmansegg: Her Moral"

10. When the English tongue we speak
    Why is "break" not rhymed with "freak"?
    Will you tell me why it's true
    We say "sew" but likewise "few";
    And the maker of a verse
    Cannot cap his horse with "worse"?
    "Beard" sounds not the same as "heard";
    "Cord" is different from "word";
    "Cow" is cow, but "low" is low;
    Shoe is never rhymed with "foe."
    Think of "hose" and "dose" and "lose";
    And of "goose"—and yet of "choose."
    Think of "comb" and "tomb" and "bomb";
    "Doll" and "roll"; and "home" and "some."
    And since "pay" is rhymed with "say"
    Why not "paid" with "said", I pray;
    We have "blood" and "food" and "good;"
    "Mould" is not pronounced like "could."
    Wherefore "done", but "gone" and "lone"?
    Is there any reason known?
    And, in short, it seems to me
    Sounds and letters disagree.
    —Anonymous

11. I am the very model of a modern Major General;
    I've information vegetable, animal and mineral;
    I know the kings of England, and I quote the fights historical,
    From Marathon to Waterloo, in order categorical.
    I'm very well acquainted, too, with matters mathematical;
    I understand equations, both simple and quadratical;
    About binomial theorem I'm teeming with a lot of news,
    With many cheerful facts about the square of the hypotenuse!
    —Gilbert and Sullivan, *H.M.S. Pinafore*

12. And the raven, never fitting,
    Still is sitting, still is sitting
    On the pallid bust of Pallas
    Just above my chamber door;
    And his eyes have all the seeming
    Of a demon's that is dreaming
    And the lamplight o'er him streaming

Throws his shadow on the floor,
And my soul from out that shadow
That lies floating on the floor
Shall be lifted nevermore.
                    —Edgar Allan Poe, "The Raven"

13. A bow-shot from her bower-eaves,
    He rode between the barley-sheaves,
    The sun came dazzling thro' the leaves,
    And flamed upon the brazen greaves
    Of bold Sir Lancelot.
                    —Alfred, Lord Tennyson, "The Lady of Shalott"

14. O, she doth teach the torches to burn bright!
    It seems she hangs upon the cheek of night
    Like a rich jewel in an Ethiop's ear;
    Beauty too rich for use, for earth too dear!
                    —William Shakespeare, *Romeo and Juliet*

15. But soft! What light through yonder window breaks?
    It is the east, and Juliet is the sun!
                    —William Shakespeare, *Romeo and Juliet*

16. Now is the winter of our discontent
    Made glorious summer by this son of York.
                    —William Shakespeare, *Richard III*

17. O, pardon me, thou bleeding piece of earth,
    That I am meek and gentle with these butchers!
    Thou art the ruins of the noblest man
    That ever lived in the tide of times.
    Woe to the hand that shed this costly blood!
                    —William Shakespeare, *Julius Caesar*

18. Make me a willow cabin at your gate,
    And call upon my soul within the house;
    Write loyal cantons of condemned love
    And sing them loud even in the dead of night;
    Halloo you name to the reverberate hills,
    And make the babbling gossip of the air
    Cry out 'Olivia!'
                    —William Shakespeare, *Twelfth Night*

19. O, that this too too solid flesh would melt,
    Thaw and resolve itself into dew!
    —William Shakespeare, *Hamlet*

20. Now is the very witching time of night
    When churchyards yawn and Hell itself breathes out contagion
    To this world.
    —William Shakespeare, *Hamlet*

21. O, what a noble mind is here o'erthrown!
    The courtier's, soldier's, scholar's, eye, tongue, sword.
    —William Shakespeare, *Hamlet*

22. Shall I compare thee to a summer's day?
    Thou art more lovely and more temperate:
    Rough winds do shake the darling buds of May,
    And summer's lease hath all too short a date;
    Sometime too hot the eye of heaven shines,
    And often is his gold complexion dimm'd;
    And every fair from fair sometime declines,
    By chance thy eternal summer shall not fade
    Nor lose possession of that fair thou ow'st;
    Nor shall Death brag thou wand'rest in his shade,
    When in eternal lines to time thou grow'st;
    So long as men can breathe or eyes can see,
    So long lives this and this gives life to thee.
    —William Shakespeare, Sonnet 18

23. When, in disgrace with fortune and men's eyes,
    I all alone beweep my outcast state,
    And trouble deaf heaven with my bootless cries,
    And look upon myself, and curse my fate,
    Wishing me like to one more rich in hope,
    Featured like him, like him with friends possess'd,
    Desiring this man's art and that man's scope,
    With what I most enjoy contented least;
    Yet in these thoughts myself most despising,
    Haply I think on thee, and then my state,
    Like to the lark at break of day arising
    From sullen earth, sings hymns at heaven's gate;
    For thy sweet love remember'd such wealth brings
    That then I scorn to change my state with kings.
    —William Shakespeare, Sonnet 29

Lesson 38
Nasal Resonance

Materials:
Nasal Resonance Worksheet (following this lesson)
mirrors

Procedure:
Today we will deal with resonance, dealing specifically with nasal resonance.

Part I:
Do some basic vocal warm-up exercises, and ask the students to hum throughout to warm up the voice. Possible exercises are spine fold, head roll, face massage (jaw joints), tongue stretchers, face tightening and expanding.

Part II:
Ask for a definition of "resonance." It is the depth and richness of the sound created by vibrations in the three resonating cavities.

Instruct them that the vibrations may also be felt throughout the facial mask, i.e., the bones around the eyes, the cheekbones, the forehead—even the top of the head! Students need to learn to "use" those vibrations to add the richness to the sound.

Do the following brief exercises, using mirrors to see mouth shapes and the movement of the uvula.

1. *Mmmm-Aahhh* (feel the vibrations in the nose on the nasal *Mmm*. Make them stronger. Open the mouth wide for the *Aahhh*. Put the sounds together—*MmmmAahhh*

2. Repeat with *Nnnn-Aahhh*

3. Sing *Song,* elongating the nasal *-ng*

4. Sing *Song* on different pitches

5. Sing *Ring-a-Ling* on different pitches. Remember to hold the *-ng* for a long time, and make it stronger as you do so.

The above exercises are for nasal resonance. Use the Nasal Resonance worksheet for practice. Each student should have the opportunity of saying one of the lines aloud, and the teacher should correct any problems. The major goal here is to try to make students appreciative of the nasals, and to hold them longer to achieve resonance.

I would like once again to reinforce the importance of listening as a way of improving the sound. I often ask students to close their eyes and concentrate on the sound in order to improve it.

Many passages may be read in unison. When specific students read well, ask the class to listen to them. This also provides positive reinforcement for the individual.

Objectives:
The student will:
- warm up the voice
- practice nasal resonance
- improve listening skills
- correct nasal resonance problems
- discuss the importance of nasal resonance in speaking for the stage

Nasal Resonance Worksheet

1. Down! Down! Down! Down!

2. Nero, the emperor, was mighty and proud!

3. The man's name

4. Manny's mama

5. Naughty Nattie came to town wearing a long and lengthy gown.

6. The magnificent ring

7. Morning's a-ringing; people a-singing

8. "Boom," barreled the mighty guns.

9. Brawling in the tavern is never unusual.

10. My mentor is never far from home.

11. Alone, alone, all, all alone.
    Alone on a wide, wide sea;
    And never a saint took pity on
    My soul in agony,
    —Samuel Taylor Coleridge, *The Rime of the Ancient Mariner*

12. Who has seen the wind?
    Neither I nor you
    But when the leaves hang trembling
    The wind is passing through.
    Who has seen the wind?
    Neither you nor I
    But when the trees bow down their heads
    The wind is passing by.
    —Christina Rossetti, "Who Has Seen the Wind?"

Lesson 39
Oral Resonance

Materials:
Articulation Worksheet (from Lesson 37)
mirrors

Procedure:
Today we will work on oral resonance.

Part I:
Same as Lesson 38.

Part II:
Students will use mirrors for the following work. Explain that resonance is achieved orally as well as nasally (the work of the previous lesson). Again, the goal of our work is to achieve depth and richness of sound.

A method of utmost importance in achieving oral resonance is to achieve correct lip shape for vowel sounds. The mouth will be open wider than it is when we speak in our typical everyday conversation. Also, the throat must be relaxed.

Students should watch you, the instructor, for the correct mouth shapes as you demonstrate. They should then attempt to re-create them as they look in the mirror.

Vowel sequence and sounds with accompanying phonetic symbols
Repeat sound and word for each:

- the "a" sound in *park*   a
- the "a" sound in *watch*   ɒ
- the "a" sound in *tall*   ɔ
- the "o" sound in *gold*   o
- the "u" sound in *took*   ʊ
- the "oo" sound in *pool*   u
- the "e" sound in *see*   i
- the "i" sound in *hill*   ɪ
- the "a" sound in *bake*   ei
- the "e" sound in *gem*   ɛ
- the "a" sound in *bad*   æ

I feel it is important to show students the phonetic symbols of these sounds also. They need to think of these units as sounds and not letters of a word.

You may want to explain purposes and reasons for the phonetic alphabet, one of which is to standardize stage speech by eliminating regionalisms.

Part III:

Use the Articulation Worksheet from Lesson 37 for class practice. Again, each student should be asked to read a passage aloud, and the teacher should correct any problems. Also, the class should read in unison.

Objectives:

The student will:
- warm up the voice
- practice oral resonance
- improve listening skills
- correct oral resonance problems
- discuss the importance of oral resonance in speaking for the stage.

Lesson 40

Excellence in Theater Voice and Speech

Materials:
a prepared tape containing excellent examples of theater voice and speech

Commentary:
I feel that these selections are best exemplified by recordings of Shakespeare and other classics. Be sure to include a good number of men *and* women, for it is important to hear the best sound from both genders. Libraries and record stores contain many of these works. A tape recorder is also needed. At this point I would warn the teacher of a potential problem in that most good Shakespeare recordings are done by British actors, and American Standard Stage Speech differs from British. This may create misconceptions about the correct way to speak Shakespearean lines. Please be advised when making the tape that numerous classical as well as contemporary recordings by American actors are available.

Procedure:
Tell the class that today they will hear examples of excellence in theater voice and speech.

Study the tape as you prepare it, jotting down specific notes and examples you want to make your students aware of. Try to focus on particularly good illustrations of resonance, as the students have worked on this in class.

Objectives:
The student will:
- listen to excellent examples of voice and speech
- identify good features of voice and speech
- improve listening skills

Part III
Scene Study

The Prime of Miss Jean Brodie by Jay Presson Allen

Photo: William Burns

Scene Study

Commentary

Scene study is of central importance to both acting courses presented in this book. All class activities—from the realistically performed simple actions of the Introductory Course to the score of sequential activities in the Advanced Course—lead in a natural progression to this all-important project.

Students are always excited about scene study. This is the closest they come in class to what they consider a "real play," and they enjoy the thrill of exploring a situation and characters created by a professional playwright. The teacher should capitalize on this built-in self-motivation by providing excellent material. A list of selected scenes from plays is included, but I've learned that the possibilities are endless, as new scenes come along rapidly.

The choice of scene is extremely important and is best done by the teacher. While the obvious purpose of scene study is to instruct through the practical application of theory, and to stretch the students' abilities, the scene should also be representative of fine dramatic literature. I personally feel that we need to find material that enables students to think, explore, and ultimately become more self-aware. Perhaps this is where "educational" theater differs from purely "professional" training.

We must therefore work to make scene study a *process* rather than merely a *product*-oriented task. It is undoubtedly wonderful to watch a polished, well-performed piece, but the actors should be encouraged to experiment and grow throughout the rehearsal period as well. For this reason I incorporate rehearsals into the classroom structure, usually two periods per week when we are immersed in our scenework unit. (This usually begins during the third week of the course, with scenes being presented during the seventh and eighth weeks. Again, this depends on the size of the class.) Scenework days offer me the opportunity of working individually with students and guiding them through the challenges presented by the various scenes.

Explanation of Charts

The charts and forms which follow are those I find quite useful in the Scene Study Unit.

Scenework Progress Chart

Since much scenework occurs during class time, I have developed a chart which holds students accountable for setting and meeting objectives each time they rehearse. The comment column is meant for students' questions, areas of concern, etc. I try to write a comment after each rehearsal period whether I have worked with those particular students or not.

Script Analysis Sheet

This sheet forces the actors to *think* about the scene rather than jumping into the acting of it immediately. Actors should know what their scenes are about and should be able to complete the sentence, "This is the story of what happens when . . ." Do not let the actors ramble. The sentence should be brief and to the point: "This is the story of what happens when a boy and a girl fall in love and their parents don't want them to be" is the story of *Romeo and Juliet*'s entire text.

Selecting an objective forces the actor to focus on exactly what he wants. He should be encouraged to go directly toward his objective. Notice that the objective is always stated in the infinitive "to _____." This forces the actor to equate the objective with action and forward-moving energy.

The climax is defined as "that moment—it can be the moment of assimilation and not necessarily a spoken word—that determines the outcome of the scene." Knowing the climax gives the actor a place in the scene toward which to "build."

Scene Evaluation Form

This is filled out after every scene's final performance. Students should be encouraged to be honest in their appraisal of each other's work. This sheet is also the basis for the oral critique which follows the performance. Please note that this form and the Self-Evaluation Form are applicable to "realistic" theater. Students may have difficulty answering questions pertaining to character believability when considering the works of such playwrights as Ionesco, Beckett, Aristophanes, etc.

Self-Evaluation Form (Acting)

I ask my students to fill out this form after they finish a scene study unit. It encourages them to evaluate their progress and gives me an insight into what they consider to be their own rate of development. These stay on file and are reviewed periodically by student and teacher.

Monologue Evaluation Form

This is similar in format to the Scene Evaluation Form.

Character Sketch Sheet

As students use this sheet, they are using both analysis and intuition. While the answers to many of the questions are found in the text (directly and by implication), the actor will need to use his creative imagination for many of them. A thorough job with this sheet will truly bring the character alive for the actor.

Scenework Progress Chart

Name ———————— Scene ————————

Date	Objective	Work Accomplished	Student Comments/Questions	Teacher Comments

Script Analysis
Sheet

Name _____ and _____

Scene _____

This is the story of what happens when _____

_____

_____

_____

Character (Name) _____ Objective: to _____

Character (Name) _____ Objective: to _____

The climax of the scene occurs on the following line or action: _____

_____

_____

If the definition of the climax is the event which determines the outcome of the scene, tell why you have chosen this line or action to serve as the climax.

_____

_____

_____

_____

_____

_____

Scene Evaluation Form

Scene taken from _____ by _____

Actor _____ Character _____

Actor _____ Character _____

1. Are the characters well-developed and believable, or are they flat and one-dimensional? Have the characters been made "human" enough to be taken out of the scene and sustain a life of their own?

2. Have appropriate choices been made in regard to dialogue and movement according to the actor's understanding of the script?

3. Is there a sense of ensemble acting? Are the actors really listening and speaking to each other and not merely reciting lines?

4. Is there enough vocal projection? Comment on diction. Is it clear, with proper attention paid to consonants and vowels? Is there variety in pitch and duration, or is it monotonous, with little change in vocal quality?

5. Are the actors properly motivating and justifying actions and feelings? Are they overdoing the emotion, or not giving it enough importance?

6. Are the actors in control at all times? Are there blatant signs of nervousness which interfere with the actors' work?

7. Have the actors analyzed the scene properly? Do they understand what the scene is about, its climax, conflict, and character objectives?

8. Have the actors made appropriate choices and effective use of costumes, props, and furniture?

Self-Evaluation Form
Acting

Use the following code in evaluating your work in the listed categories:

1. Satisfactory
2. Fair, but could use improvement
3. An area of concern
4. Not applicable

Characterization

_____ I create a believable character—one that is not flat and one-dimensional, but human enough to be taken out of the scene and sustain a life of his/her own.

_____ I "get into" the character, feeling comfortable with the motivation and justification of feelings and ideas.

_____ I truly talk and listen to fellow actors on stage.

_____ I can determine the proper amount of emotion needed for the scene.

Voice

_____ The voice quality selected helps determine the character's age and background/lifestyle.

Vocal Elements

_____ Projection

_____ Diction

        _____ I pay proper attention to initial and ending sounds of words.

_____ Pitch

_____ Duration

_____ Variety

_____ Tempo

Body

_____ The physicality chosen creates the age and background/life-style of the character.

_____ I feel comfortable with the business of the scene.

Blocking

_____ The blocking contributes to the effect and reflects the interpretation of the scene.

_____ The blocking is varied and not monotonous.

_____ Both vertical and horizontal blocking is used.

_____ There is good use of levels.

_____ All areas of the stage are used.

_____ The aesthetic weight is evenly distributed.

Props, Set, Costumes

_____ My use of props is justified and motivated.

_____ Props are an "extension" of my body and not artificial.

_____ I have endowed my props with a "life of their own."

_____ The set created for the scene contributes to the effect and reflects the interpretation of the scene.

_____ The costume selected (style, color, period) is appropriate for the character and for the intent/interpretation of the scene.

Analysis

_____ I can determine the "story" of the scene ("This is the story of what happens when . . .")

_____ I can determine the objective of my character.

_____ I can determine the climax of the scene

Preparation

_____ I use the class time allotted for scenework well.

_____ I devote sufficient "outside" time to scene preparation, either alone or with my partner.

_____ I apply classroom theory to the preparation and performance of my scene.

_____ I research the historical period of the scene (major events, social and economic conditions, lifestyles, manner of dress, movements, etc.).

General Evaluation

_____ I felt comfortable with my performance.

_____ Nervousness did not work against the performance of my scene.

_____ I was satisfied with the performance.

Comments:

Monologue Evaluation Form

Actor _____ Scene _____

Responder _____

1. Monologues are often more difficult than scenes for two or more actors because less is spoken, yet similar amounts of information need to be communicated. Considering this, is the character well-developed and believable, or is it flat and one-dimensional?

2. Who is the character talking to?

3. Can you determine the intention of the character? the reason for sharing this information with the audience or another character?

4. Monologues depend upon vocal variety and an "orchestrated" voice. Is there enough variety in this piece? What about *diction* and *projection?*

5. Is there enough movement and business in this scene? Is there too much? What would you suggest for blocking/business?

6. Are there blatant signs of nervousness which interfere with the actor's work?

7. Has the actor made appropriate choices and effective use of costumes, props, and furniture?

8. Did this scene "work" for you? Why or why not?

Character Sketch Sheet

I. Physical Silhouette

- character's age, weight, height
- type of speech
- characteristic way of walking
- particular mannerisms or idiosyncracies
- nationality, section of the country
- level of vitality

II. Character Biography

- childhood, adolescence, middle age, old age
- educational background
- occupation
- hobbies
- home life
- social life
- style of dress
- level of IQ

III. Psychological Silhouette

- What is the character's environment like?
- What is his/her self-concept (the way he/she sees self)?
- How does the character behave under emotional stress? (reactions to love, fear, anger, jealousy)
- What is the character's outlook on life (basically optimistic or pessimistic)?

IV. Sensory or Physical Images (if you were, what would you be?)

- animal
- flower
- house
- color
- music
- type of beverage
- season of the year
- odor
- type of furniture
- type of transportation
- type of literature
- household implement

V. Play Structure and Analysis

- Is your character sympathetic or unsympathetic (how is the audience to line up with the character)?
- What is the type of play (comedy, tragedy, variant)?
- Where is the crisis in the play (climax in the character)?
- What is your relationship to *each* of the other characters (which like you, which do not)?
- Is the character well-rounded or somewhat diluted by the playwright's intention?
- What changes take place in the character? (actor *must* reveal progression in the character's development. How is he/she different at the end of the play from behavior at the beginning?)

VI. Objectives

- What is the character's super-objective (overall goal)?
- What is the objective of each scene (specific objective)?

Some further questions you may want to answer in

Tackling a Role

- What are you? What do you do in life?
- What do you want out of life?
- What does the character do to get what he/she wants out of life?
- What is your relationship to other characters? What do you feel towards them?
- What do other characters say about you? Are they truthful?
- Why do they react to you as they do?
- What are your likes and dislikes?
- What do you say? How do you express yourself?
- What actions are implied in your lines?
- What are your beliefs and convictions?
- Are there any special stage directions that offer clues to your goal?

Always keep in mind: What is your goal? You must be motivated in every action you take, in every statement you make.

Post-Performance Critique

One of the most important, difficult, and sensitive components of an acting class is the post-performance discussion/critique. When properly conducted, it serves as an exciting learning tool; when improperly conducted it can be a humiliating, anti-educational experience. Finesse and tact are of utmost importance in making students feel good about their efforts, while identifying and correcting those areas which need attention.

I encourage the class to participate in post-performance critique because I feel it is important for students to be actively involved. Also, the critique can and should be as valuable for the class as it is for the actor.

The following, then, is a guide for the post-performance critique.

First and foremost, the teacher should build an atmosphere of trust and respect, what Madeline Hunter refers to as "feeling tone." Actually, this atmosphere should be initiated from the very first day of class. Students should feel comfortable in an acting class, because they know that they are respected and valued for their differences. One of the many joys of performance is that it provides many ways to achieve a desired goal or effect. For example, the outward signs of such emotions as love, anger, fear, and grief will be different depending on who is performing and what the circumstances are. Assign the same scene to two or more groups of actors and compare the results. Each actor, as long as he is truthful to himself and the text, is "correct."

Such diversity is an asset for the critique session, for it encourages students to explore options (and makes others aware of options they had not realized before), and make choices. It even affords them the opportunity to "fail" in their attempts to discover—something they don't get too often. What better way to grow? What better way to become more self-aware? And isn't self-awareness a significant part of what acting is all about?

The first part of the critique is nonjudgmental. It deals with the "world" of the performance, whether that performance is a scene from the scene-study unit or any exercise in the curriculum. Ask students to respond to what they "saw." Ask questions like "How did the set make you feel?" "What mood was created by the costumes, props, lighting (if any)?" The actor may respond here as to whether this was or was not the intended effect.

Next, ask the class what they liked about the performance. What worked? What was effective? This support/praise will make the student feel positive about his work by noting in public real achievements and accomplishments. It is important for the actor to know that the delivery of a line he worked on for so long did indeed have an impact, or that the class truly empathized with a particular moment of the performance. This positive reaction will lead the actor to seek ways to become even stronger, and he will therefore pay greater attention as you, the teacher, focus on areas that need attention.

Needless to say, the trust between student and teacher should never be broken. Neither should the teacher nor the class hunt for or fabricate positive comments; false or phony praise is itself a violation of trust, and a form of dishonesty. If that point is reached, it is probably better to ask the student to rework the material and present it at a future time.

The third part of the critique deals with correcting the actor's problems. While it is never difficult to find numerous mistakes in the work of a student actor, select one, or perhaps two basic problems and make him aware of them. An area of concern may deal with imagery, or believable sensory recall, or even basic blocking. To overwhelm an actor with his mistakes is detrimental to effective learning. I sometimes videotape the scenes when they are performed. Playback of the tape during this or the work session is valuable, enabling the actors to actually see or hear the areas in question.

One other note about the critique session that the teacher—especially one who has not experienced this before—should be prepared for: While this session is most often a true sharing of ideas that are creative, unique, and dynamic, the very nature of the theater encourages sublimation and identification on the part of the audience. Class members may talk about the feelings, circumstances, and events of a given scene as they apply to their own lives. While this is a positive reaction and an aim of major productions, the class critique session cannot spend too much time with such discussion. The teacher must guide the session forward, allowing class time for valuable input, yet affording emphasis to the work of the actors.

The last part of the critique is the work session, which can be as brief or as long as the instructor needs to make the actor aware of and correct the problem. The methodology of this work session is derived from the acting teacher's training. There is no one way to bring out the best in one's students. Rather, the correction of problems must take into account what both the actor and the teacher feel most comfortable with, and those, in turn, are dependent upon the various learning styles. One suggestion is to "talk through" the problem. Another is to ask the actor(s) to re-enact a segment of the scene and have the teacher direct it, making more appropriate choices. Yet another method is to view the videotape mentioned above. These strategies aim to correct problems by suggesting new options to the student actor, and stretch him to reach new potentials or discover new abilities.

Students and teacher should feel good about the post-performance critique. Accomplishments are valued; positive aspects of the performance are reinforced; problems are corrected. True growth occurs.

Scenes for Practice
Introduction to Acting

Play	Author	Characters	Act/Scene	Dialogue
A Hatful of Rain	Michael Gazzo	2m	II, ii	Johnny: "Polo! Hi" *to* Polo: "You can't win. They'll kick your ribs in."
The Matchmaker	Thornton Wilder	1m, 1f	III	Vandergelder: "Where are you going?" *to* Mrs. Levi: "I say another word either." (Two additional small roles may be cut.)
Teach Me How to Cry	Patricia Joudry	2f	II, ii	Polly: "Your mother will be all right, Melinda" *to* Polly: "You slut!"
Butterflies Are Free	Leonard Gershe	2f		Mrs. Baker: "Mrs. Benson!" *to* Jill: "Too bad. She's really very nice."
The Rise and Rise of Daniel Rocket	Peter Parnell	1m, 1f	I, viii	Daniel: "Don't close it, Alice" *to* end of scene.
Liliom	Ferenc Molnar	2f	I	Marie: "Are you sorry for him?" *to* Julie: "He's nothing but a common porter."
Enter Laughing	Joseph Stein	1m, 1f	I, v	Angela: "Entrez!" *to* David: "You're a better man than I, Gunga Din!"
A Roomful of Roses	Edith Sommer	2f		Bridget: "I don't know why everybody gets so excited . . ." *to* Bridget: "You're crazy."

Play	Author	Characters	Act/Scene	Dialogue
The Diary of Anne Frank	Frances Goodrich and Albert Hackett	1m, 1f	II, iv	Anne: "Look, Peter, the sky," *to* Anne: "Some day, when we're outside again, I'm going to . . ."
Pygmalion	George Bernard Shaw	2f	II	Mrs. Pearce: "I will have to put you here" *to* Eliza: "I didn't know when I was well off."
Career	James Lee	1m, 1f	I	Barbara: "Two hundred dollars!" *to* Barbara: " . . . so happy in the history of the world."

Psychophysical Scenes (Dramatic)

Advanced Acting

Play	Author	Characters	Act/Scene	Dialogue
All My Sons	Arthur Miller	1m, 1f	I	Chris: "Isn't he a great guy?" *to* Ann: "What'll I do with a fortune?"
Antigone	Jean Anouilh	2f	one act	Ismene: "Antigone! What are you doing up at this hour?" *to* Antigone: "Poor Ismene."
The Crucible	Arthur Miller	1m, 1f	bet. II & III	Proctor: "I must speak with you, Abigail." *to* Abigail: "From yourself I will save you."
Desire Under the Elms	Eugene O'Neill	1m, 1f	Part II, Sc. 2 & 3	Part two from Abbie's entrance to Eben's room *to* end of scene; all of scene 3.
The Diary of Anne Frank	Frances Goodrich and Albert Hackett	1m, 1f	II, ii	Anne: "Aren't they awful?" *to* Anne's exit.
A Doll's House	Henrick Ibsen	1m, 1f	I	Nora: "You want to speak to me?" *to* Krogstad: " . . . you shall keep me company."
Golden Boy	Clifford Odets	1m, 1f	II, ii	Joe: "Some nights I wake up . . ." *to* Joe: "Poor Lorna."
A Hatful of Rain	Michael Gazzo	1m, 1f	I, i	Celia: "There's no hot water, is there?" *to* Celia: "Everything's so damp in here."

Play	Author	Characters	Act/Scene	Dialogue
Home of the Brave	Arthur Laurents	2m	II, ii	Coney: "78-77-76-75" *to* Doctor: "All right, son! All right!"
I Never Sang for My Father	Robert Anderson	1m, 1f	Act II	Alice: "I don't know how you feel." *to* Gene: "I've always wanted to love him."
Isn't It Romantic?	Wendy Wasserstein	2f	I, v	Harriet: "So, what do you think?" *to* Janie: " . . . throwing out the garbage?"
The Little Foxes	Lillian Hellman	2f	III	Regina: "What do you want to talk to me about, Alexandra?" *to* Alexandra: "Are you afraid, mother?"
Look Back in Anger	John Osborne	2f	III, ii	Alison: "He still smokes that foul old stuff . . ." *to* Helena: " . . . and I've got to tell him now."
A Man for All Seasons	Robert Bolt	2m	I	Wolsey: "It's half past one . . ." *to* More: "Like yourself, Your Grace?"
Middle of the Night	Paddy Chayefsky	1m, 1f	III, i	The Girl: "George, I'd like to know why you came back," *to* The Husband: "I swear I won't do it again."
Picnic	William Inge	1m, 1f	III, i	Howard: "Here we are, honey . . ." *to* Rosemary's exit.
The Prime of Miss Jean Brodie	Jay Presson Allen	1m, 1f	III, ii	Entire scene
The Rainmaker	N. Richard Nash	1m, 1f	II	Starbuck: "Who's that? Who's there" *to* end of act

227

Psychophysical Scenes (Dramatic)

Advanced Acting—continued

Play	Author	Characters	Act/Scene	Dialogue
The Shadow Box	Michael Cristofer	1m, 1f	II	Joe: "A farm would have been nice." *to* Joe: "Just come inside."
The Sign in Sidney Brustein's Window	Lorraine Hansberry	1m, 1f	II, ii	Sidney: "You know what, the craziest thing is happening to Wally" *to* Iris's exit.
Stage Door	Edna Ferber and George S. Kaufman	2f	I, ii	Kaye: "I know how sunk you feel, Terry," *to* Terry: "Life rolls right along for her."
Summer and Smoke	Tennessee Williams	1m, 1f	Scene 6	Entire scene
Tea and Sympathy	Robert Anderson	1m, 1f	II, ii	Laura: "I've been expecting you" *to* Laura: "Tom! Tom!"

Comedy Scenes

Advanced Acting

Play	Author	Characters	Act/Scene	Dialogue
Ah, Wilderness!	Eugene O'Neill	1m, 1f	IV, ii	Richard's entrance *to* Richard: "It felt wonderful even to have you bite."
Barefoot in the Park	Neil Simon	1m, 2f	I	Paul: "Hello, Mom." *to* Corie: "I'll be the judge of who's happy."
Barefoot in the Park	Neil Simon	1m, 1f	I	Paul: "Corie . . . where are you?" *to* Corie: "But it's my mother."
Blithe Spirit	Noel Coward	1m, 1f	I, ii	Ruth: "Well, darling?" *to* Elvira: "To hell with Ruth."
Blithe Spirit	Noel Coward	2f	II, ii	Madam Arcati: "My dear Mrs. Condomine, I came directly" *to* Madam Arcati: " . . . stew in your own juices."
Born Yesterday	Garson Kanin	1m, 1f	II	Beginning of act *to* Brock's entrance (scene can be shortened)
Brighton Beach Memoirs	Neil Simon	2f	I	Laurie: "So what are you going to do?" *to* Nora: "I'll go with you Saturday."
Crimes of the Heart	Beth Henley	2f	I	Lenny: "Hello . . . oh hello, Lucille" *to* Lenny: "They're home, Meg!"

Comedy Scenes

Advanced Acting—continued

Play	Author	Characters	Act/Scene	Dialogue
The Gingerbread Lady	Neil Simon	2f	II	Polly: (on phone) "Hello? Is this Joe Allen's?" *to* Evy: "I should have had two sherries today."
The Good Doctor	Neil Simon	2m, 1f	II, iii	Entire scene
The Goodbye People	Herb Gardner	1m, 1f	II	Arthur: "Oh. . . ." *to* Nancy: "Take it easy, we've got plenty to talk about."
Hobson's Choice	Harold Brighouse	1m, 1f	I	Maggy: "Willie, come here" *to* Willie: "Ada would tell another story, though."
The Importance of Being Earnest	Oscar Wilde	2f	II	Cecily: "Pray let me introduce myself to you." *to* Cecily: ". . . other calls of a similar character to make in the neighborhood."
Lovers and Other Strangers	Joseph Bologna and Renee Taylor	1m, 1f	ii	Entire scene

Play	Author	Characters	Act/Scene	Dialogue
The Odd Couple	Neil Simon	2m	II, i	Felix: "That's funny, isn't it, Oscar?" *to* Felix: "The girls'll be crazy about it."
The Owl and the Pussycat	Bill Manhoff	1m, 1f	I	Doris: "God damn it! Hey fink, fink!" *to* Doris: "It makes me mad as hell!"
The Philadelphia Story	Philip Barry	1m, 1f	II	Tracy: "Did you enjoy the party?" *to* Tracy: "put me in your pocket, Mike."
Prisoner of Second Avenue	Neil Simon	1m, 1f	I, i	Edna: (on phone) "Edison, Mrs. Edna Edison" *to* Mel: "Dirty bastards!"
Rhinoceros	Eugène Ionesco	2m	II, ii	Jean: "What is it?" *to* Berenger: "Get the police!"
6 RMS Riv Vu	Bob Randall	1m, 1f	II, i	Paul: "Sing it, baby" *to* Paul: "I see a parking space!"
Thieves	Herb Gardner	1m, 1f	I	Sally: "Can I ask you a question?" *to* Sally: " . . . you were a goddamn interesting person."

The Crucible by Arthur Miller

Relaxation/Warm-Up Exercises for the Actor

Commentary

At the core of all fine acting is a *relaxed* body and voice, free from the daily tensions which prevent us from doing our best on the stage. Too often actors, in their enthusiasm, merely want to take to the stage and perform without adequately warming up. The voice and the body are parts of what should be a finely tuned machine, and they must be ready to provide the maximum flexibility to meet the rigorous demands of the stage. It would be difficult to imagine a well-trained dancer or singer performing without first exercising. Likewise, we need to teach our students that acting is an *art* and we need to treat our "instrument" with the same respect that other artists treat theirs.

This is part of the "discipline" I mentioned in the Introduction. Eager and excited people who view the theater as a place for fun only often tend to miss the structure behind it, the need for a serious, systematic, and logical approach to their work. I'm afraid that students often respond to the word *structure* with suspicion. They think of it as "limiting" or "restrictive," as setting perimeters within which one must remain. Actually, it is this very structure which affords a tremendous amount of flexibility and experimentation. Relaxation/Warm-Up Exercises make actors *more* creative and spontaneous, and they certainly charge rehearsals, performances, and classes with vibrancy and excitement.

I use Relaxation/Warm-Up Exercises before every rehearsal for about 20 to 30 minutes, and before performances for about 45 minutes. I also often use them for a few minutes at the beginning of classes. The benefits of these exercises are many and varied, and they are often not limited to the theater. Many former students over the past twenty-five and more years reiterate the important role theater exercises still play in their lives. They have been used in the sales and advertising fields before delivering that big "pitch" in the boardroom, and they have been used by school teachers and administrators while handling conflicts, crises, or just an inordinate amount of paperwork; they have been used by therapists during a stressful day dealing with clients, and they have even been used by youthful aspirants prior to a job interview.

My eyes were first "opened" to exercising when I studied with the late great acting teacher Constance Welch. In our Stage Speaking Class, Miss Welch put us through the rigors of what seemed a very strange ordeal at the time. We "shook out" and stretched; we "scrunched up" and expanded. We learned also that exercising is at once physical *and* mental, and that the mind benefited from the body's workout as well. And soon we noticed a distinct and wonderful difference in our work on the stage. We were more responsive and aware; we reacted to stimuli in ways that surprised and thrilled us; we relished a new spontaneity in our work. We felt truly liberated!

Many of the exercises which follow originated in that class with Miss Welch. Many are new. Exercises tend to change over the years, and new ones are constantly added to the repertoire. All, however, play a central role in the training of an actor; all are certainly beneficial in ordinary, day-to-day activity.

A Typical Warm-Up Exercise Session

A typical warm-up session is divided into two parts: exercises for the body and those for the voice. The former is divided into exercises for:

- the upper body
- the lower body
- the whole body
- the head and neck
- the face

Voice exercises deal with proper breathing and articulation. These areas are covered in detail in the Advanced Acting Course in this book. I refer you to these lessons when selecting material for this area of the exercise session.

As I worked on this section of *Lessons for the Stage,* my mind was flooded with numerous additional exercises. I had to resist the temptation of including more—many of which are wonderful!—in keeping with my original goal of presenting a basic core, which comprise a "typical" warm-up session. Please feel free to augment this list with exercises of your own. As long as you deal with the major divisions described above, variety will add interest and enthusiasm to this crucial element of an actor's training.

I ask the actors to hum during the body exercises in order to warm up the vocal cords for the voice part of the exercise session. I also direct the actors to take several deep breaths during the session to meet the body's need for increased amounts of oxygen. You may also want to play soft music as the group exercises to help in the relaxation process.

The Upper Body

Hands and Arms: Shake out the fingers very well. Next, shake out from the wrists. Follow this by shaking out from the elbows. Next, include both arms, from the shoulder to the tips of the fingers. The shake-outs should be vigorously performed. Now, with your feet set a foot or so apart, twist at the waist and allow the arms to sway loosely at your sides.

Shoulders and Neck: Raise your right shoulder gently to your right ear and let it fall (do not "push" it down). Raise your left shoulder and let it fall. Now raise both shoulders and let them fall. Repeat this five or six times. This relaxes the neck and shoulder muscles.

Shoulders: We continue to work with the shoulders by rotating the right shoulder backward in large circular movements. Change directions and rotate it forward. Do the same with the left shoulder. Then do both shoulders simultaneously.

The Lower Body

Feet: Raise your right knee and shake out the ankle. This exercise is more difficult than it sounds, for the foot must be totally relaxed. Imagine controlling the shake-out from the ankle, with everything below the ankle dead weight. Repeat with the left ankle.

Legs: With feet set approximately three feet apart and hands on hips, stretch to the right. Hold the stretch for a moment. Now stretch to the left. Return to the starting position, and with the feet remaining basically where they were for the previous stretches, turn the body (including the feet) to the right and stretch forward. You will need to place a hand on the right thigh for support. Now do the same to the left. Shake out the legs a bit to relax the muscles after this exercise.

Hips and Pelvis: With your feet spread apart on the floor and your hands on your hips, rotate your hips in full circles to the right. Change directions after a while. Next, rotate them in a figure-eight. Return to full circles.

The Whole Body

Whole Body: The spine fold is truly one of the best exercises to do for relaxation. If an actor has very little time to exercise before a rehearsal, or if you need a quick relaxation exercise before class, I strongly recommend this one.

Stand with your feet approximately a foot apart. Your body should be aligned and your arms hanging comfortably at your sides. Begin to bend over, starting with the head. Let the head completely relax, with the chin touching the neck, before you begin to include the neck in the fold over. With the head relaxed, begin at the base of the skull—where the head and neck join—and feel the tension drain from one vertebra at a time. This tension drain should continue down each vertebra in the spinal column until you are bent over from the waist. Bend your knees slightly to relieve any pressure in the small of the back. The head should be hanging down with the neck elongated from the natural force of gravity.

Once down, add a slight bounce. Pivot, with the feet stationary, to the right, then back to center, then to the left, and then back to center. Begin to ascend *slowly,* one vertebra at a time, until you are totally erect. Remember to treat the shoulders, neck, and head as separate entities rather than bringing them up together. When this exercise is done slowly, the results are relaxing and refreshing.

The Head and Neck

Head and Neck: Roll the head gently to the right, back, left, and down, creating a circular movement. Again, do this exercise slowly. Sometimes students observe that the head-roll exercise is uncomfortable when the head is in the back position. This is often due to pushing the head too far backward. Encourage students to relax with this exercise, for it is an excellent one for the neck muscles. Please note that students should be humming through this exercise as they have been doing throughout the entire session. When the head is in the back position of the head roll, however, the mouth should open slightly to prevent strain on the throat. The hum then becomes an "Aaaahhhh" for this position in the circular movement of the head.

Neck: Standing in an aligned position, turn the head to the right. Be sure that the chin remains parallel to the ground during the movement. Turn the head through the original center position and continue to the left. Complete seven or eight head turns to each side. The movement must always remain smooth with the chin parallel to the floor.

The Face

Lips and Cheeks: Press the lips together and smile broadly. Next, purse the lips tightly. Follow this with opening the mouth wide. Return to pursing the lips and then smiling once again. Repeat this several times as we begin to stimulate the facial muscles.

Forehead, Nose, and Eyes: Close your eyes and tighten your forehead. This will also include your eyes and nose. Expand it by lifting your eyebrows high. Repeat this two or three times

Entire Face: Tighten your entire face—forehead, eyes, cheeks, nose, lips, etc. Expand the face as wide as possible. Repeat this a few times. You will feel a delightful "tingle" in the facial muscles.

Afterword

I first met Julian Schlusberg at a parent-teacher conference because he was a teacher of my youngest son. That child, Joshua, praised Schlusberg without cease. My wife and I decided to check him out, and we soon discovered why Josh was so enthusiastic. Schlusberg was a parents' teacher: firm but kind, compassionate, informed and devoted. He had endeared himself to Josh and a host of fellow students by his teaching of acting and his directing of plays. This was in the early 1970s and any parent at that troubled time yearned for benign forces that would help to keep his child from ruination. Schlusberg nonchalantly, effectively, efficiently, and eloquently became that force. When I was asked to write this afterword, I immediately accepted with gratitude, not just for myself but for all of us parents in Hamden, Connecticut, who owe Schlusberg an enormous debt. He helped to save our children by his talent, his dedication, his intelligence, and his sympathy. Finally I have a chance to thank him in print. The spirit and talent that I met in person some twenty-odd years ago is the same talent and person, the same spirit, that wrote this book.

I have seen dozens of productions that Julian Schlusberg has directed; I have been a judge of competitions in which he has participated; I have lectured his fellow teachers at conferences, and talked to a great number of students who graduated from his classes. All these experiences give testimony to his outstanding ability to communicate *skills* to acting students and to draw out of those young people whatever talent resides within. He *knows* acting, has an unsentimental attachment to that craft, and he knows people—especially young people. I have just retired after almost forty years of university teaching, and I know that many of us forget how young people feel and think. It takes considerable imagination and an abundance of smarts to go back and recall what is going on with young people from the age of thirteen to adulthood. To teach them something about acting requires not only placing yourself in their shoes, but doing so without pretension, without judgment, without generalizing, without fantasizing. One must do it specifically, genuinely, and intelligently. You don't have to indulge or exaggerate; you don't have to sentimentalize or revere; but you *do* have to honor what is happening to a person in those difficult years of confusion, bewilderment, and frustration. To teach people of those years successfully, one must have a remarkable sense of balance and an unrelenting sense of mission. These are the kinds of abilities with which Schlusberg is blessed. He can *really* do it, whereas most of us are limited to trying to do it.

The director Peter Brook has said that the function of the theater is to make the invisible visible. And the purpose of acting training is precisely to release the actor to make that which is invisible in the human being visible to the audience. The teacher touches those secrets, those vulnerable and hidden areas of the students' psyches, and with that touch frees the student to apply craft to the expression of those deep recesses. That is the kind of training that makes for believable expression, credible acting, which can provide for an audience that magic which comes from accomplished performing. To reach the height of those depths requires patience, training, and courage.

Such training is as valuable in many respects for the human being of any age as it is for the actor. In fact, I would consider it essential to a person for the living of the best possible life, and absolutely necessary to the actor in order to nurture the best possible career. Schlusberg is as concerned for the human being as he is for the actor. His exercises help a student, whatever that student's interest, become a more accomplished person. These exercises require the student to listen, to look, to see, and to feel sympathy, even empathy. They test the student's vulnerability, ethical habits of action, personal consideration, and ability to take imaginative leaps. Drama is an art form in which characters are constantly being tested. The training that Schlusberg encourages carries out the regiment of testing, the drama of acting. His courses require toughness and tenderness, fear and courage, wisdom and foolishness. They simply require all those contradictory qualities with which our daily lives are imbued.

People know most everything in the way of emotional life by the time they are five. The years which follow put rust over all those feelings, and we spend much of our lives trying to get the rust off. Acting training is one means of removing the rust. It is healthy for all of us, but it requires considerable bravery. As actors we put ourselves into other lives, feeling what another person might be enjoying or suffering. As such, we are expanding our horizons significantly. We are getting *out* of ourselves in order to get *closer* to ourselves. What could be a more human activity! We learn to hear one another, to look at one another, to feel for one another. And when we are young, as are many students who will use this book, we are especially so preoccupied with *our own* feelings and thoughts, that we have to be pressed intensely to fight our way into the reality of another human being.

As a teacher of acting and as the author of this book, Julian

Schlusberg reminds me of the playwright Chekhov. Chekhov was a doctor blessed with the capacity to see the patient and the disease—to integrate patient and disease as one would integrate heart and mind, to see the disease in one patient *only*. Such a gift is peculiar to the very rare physician as it is to the very rare teacher. To see the individual student; to concentrate on that particular person; to honor the identity of each individual is a yeoman task. I don't know if such a gift can be taught. At any rate, in acting training as in all the arts, as much is to be caught as is to be taught. One must provide fertile ground for the student to catch and surprise both herself or himself and the instructor.

A teacher cannot give students the ability to catch. The teacher *can,* however, provide the environment in which the student can catch. And no teacher knows what a student will learn from what the teacher teaches. Robert Lewis, a brilliant teacher of acting, required the students at Yale University to come to every class—not because of vanity or some rule or regulation, but because he didn't know what the student would hear *that day* that might make a difference in the actor's life.

One never knows what a person as actor or simply as a human being might pick up from a teacher or a colleague. One never knows what is being caught, although one might believe that he or she knows what is being taught. This book has provided such an atmosphere and environment. You have had the luxurious opportunity to catch a rising star.

Howard Stein
Professor Emeritus
Columbia University

Bibliography

General Sources

Albright, Hardie. *Stage Direction in Transition*. Encino, CA, and Belmont, CA: Dickinson Publishing Co., 1972.

Barton, Arthur. *The Director's Voice, Twenty-one Interviews*. New York, NY: Theatre Communications Group, 1988.

Benedetti, Robert L. *The Actor at Work*. Englewood Cliffs, NJ: Prentice Hall, 1981.

Berry, Cecily. *The Actor and His Text*. London: HARRAP Ltd., 1987.

Boleslavski, Richard. *Acting, the First Six Lessons*. New York, NY: Theater Arts Books, 1933.

Chekhov, Michael. *To the Actor on the Technique of Acting*. New York, NY: Harper and Row, 1953.

Clurman, Harold. *On Directing*. New York, NY: Collier Books, 1972.

Cohen, Robert. *Acting Power*. Palo Alto, CA: Mayfield Publishing Co., 1978.

Cole, Toby, and Helen Krich Chinoy. *Directors on Directing*. New York, NY: Holt, Rinehart and Winston, 1941.

Crawford, Jerry L., and Joan Snyder. *Acting in Person and in Style*. Dubuque, IO: William C. Brown Co., 1976.

Dean, Alexander, and Lawrence Carra. *Fundamentals of Play Directing*. New York, NY: Holt, Rinehart and Winston, 1941.

Dezseran, Louis John. *The Student Actor's Handbook*. Palo Alto, CA: Mayfield Publishing Co., 1975.

Easty, Edward Dwight. *On Method Acting*. Florence, AL: House Collectibles, 1966.

Felheim, Marvin. *Comedy: Plays, Theory, and Criticism*. New York, NY: Harcourt, Brace and World, 1962.

Hagen, Uta. *Respect for Acting*. New York, NY: Macmillan Publishing Co., 1973.

Herman, Lewis and Marguerite. *American Dialects, A Manual for Actors, Directors, and Writers*. New York, NY: Theater Arts Books, 1947.

Klein, Maxine. *Time, Space, and Designs for Actors*. Boston, MA: Houghton Mifflin, 1975.

Linklater, Kristin. *Freeing the Natural Voice*. New York, NY: Drama Book Specialists, 1976.

Machlin, Evangeline. *Speech for the Stage*. New York, NY: Theater Arts Books, 1966.

Manderino, Ned. *The Transparent Actor*. Los Angeles, CA: Ned Manderino Associates, 1976.

McGaw, Charles. *Acting Is Believing.* New York, NY: Holt, Rinehart and Winston, 1966.

Meckler, Eva. *The New Generation of Acting Teachers.* New York, NY: Viking Penguin, 1987.

Moore, Sonia. *Training an Actor.* New York, NY: Viking, 1968.

Morris, Eric. *Irreverent Acting.* New York, NY: Perigee Books, 1985.

Morris, Eric, and Joan Hotchkis. *No Acting Please.* Los Angeles, CA: Whitehouse/Spelling Publications, 1977.

Poisson, Camille L. *Theater and The Adolescent Actor: Building a Successful School Program.* Hamden, CT: The Shoe String Press, 1994.

Rockwood, Jerome. *The Craftsmen of Dionysus, an Approach to Acting.* Glenview, IL: Scott, Foresman and Co., 1966.

Russell, Douglas A. *Period Style for the Theatre.* Boston, MA: Allyn and Bacon, 1987.

Skinner, Edith Warman. *Speak with Distinction.* New Brunswick, NJ: Edith Warman Skinner, 1965.

Stanislavsky, Constantin. *Building a Character,* trans. Elizabeth Reynolds Hapgood. New York, NY: Theatre Arts Books, 1949.

———. *My Life in Art,* trans. G. Ivanov-Mumjiev. Moscow: Foreign Language Publishing House, no date given.

White, Edwin C., and Marguerite Battye. *Acting and Stage Movement.* New York, NY: Arco Publishing Co., 1963.

Willis, Robert J., ed. *The Director in a Changing Theatre.* Palo Alto, CA: Mayfield Publishing Co., 1976.

Scene Study Sources

Beard, Jocelyn A., ed. *The Best Women's Stage Monologues of 1991.* Newbury, VT: Smith and Kraus, 1992.

———. *The Best Men's Stage Monologues of 1991.* Newbury, VT: Smith and Kraus, 1992.

Beard, Jocelyn A., and Kristin Graham. *The Best Scenes for Men from the 1980's.* Newbury, VT: Smith and Kraus, 1991.

The Best Scenes for Women from the 1980's. Newbury, VT: Smith and Kraus, 1991.

Earley, Michael, and Phillipa Keil, eds. *Solo! The Best Monologues of the 80's (Men).* New York, NY: Applause Theatre Books Publishers, 1987.

———. *Solo! The Best Monologues of the 80's (Women).* New York, NY: Applause Theatre Books Publishers, 1987.

———. *Soliloquy: The Shakespeare Monologues, the Men.* New York, NY: Applause Theatre Books Publishers, 1988.

———. *Soliloquy: The Shakespeare Monologues, the Women.* New York, NY: Applause Theatre Books Publishers, 1988.

Elkind, Samuel. *28 Scenes for Acting Practice.* Glenview, IL: Scott, Foresman and Co., 1971.

———. *30 Scenes for Acting Practice.* Glenview, IL: Scott, Foresman and Co., 1972.

———. *32 Scenes for Acting Practice.* Glenview, IL: Scott, Foresman and Co., 1972.

Emerson, Robert, and Jane Grumbach, eds. *Monologues Men: 50 Speeches from the Contemporary Theatre.* New York, NY: Drama Book Publishers, 1976.

———. *Monologues Men II: 50 Speeches from the Contemporary Theatre.* New York, NY: Drama Book Publishers, 1983.

———. *Monologues Women: 50 Speeches from the Contemporary Theatre.* New York, NY: Drama Book Publishers, 1976.

———. *Monologues Women II: 50 Speeches from the Contemporary Theatre.* New York, NY: Drama Book Publishers, 1982.

Greenslade, Mary, and Anne Harvey, eds. *Scenes for Two, Book II, Duologues for Girls and Women.* New York, NY,: Samuel French, no date given.

Handman, Wynn, ed. *Modern American Scenes for Student Actors.* New York, NY: Bantam Books, 1978.

Karshner, Roger, ed. *Monologues from the Classics: Shakespeare, Marlowe, and Others.* Toluka Lake, CA: Dramaline Publishers, 1986.

Lane, Eric, and Nina Shengold, eds. *The Actor's Book of Scenes from New Plays.* New York, NY: Viking Penguin, 1988.

Lane, Ruth. *Scenebook for Student Actors.* Belmont, CA: Wadsworth Publishing Co., 1973.

Pike, Frank, and Thomas G. Dunn. *Scenes and Monologues from the New American Theater.* New York, NY: Mentor, 1988.

Rudnicki, Stefan, ed. *Classical Monologues: 1, Shakespeare.* New York, NY: Drama Book Specialists, 1979.

———. *Classical Monologues: 2, Shakespeare and Friends.* New York, NY: Drama Book Specialists, 1980.

Schulman, Michael, and Eva Meckler, eds. *The Actor's Scenebook: Scenes and Monologues from Contemporary Plays.* New York, NY,: Bantam Books, 1984.

———. *The Actor's Scenebook: Scenes and Monologues from Contemporary Plays, Volume II.* New York NY,: Bantam Books, 1987.

———. *Contemporary Scenes for Student Actors.* New York, NY: Penguin Books, 1980.